THE
HEART
RESET

A Woman's Guide to Healing and
Finding Extraordinary Love
After Divorce

Madison P Kirksey

For more information, email theauthormadison@gmail.com.

Dedication

To my son Brock

You were already making me a better person before you were born. You gave me the courage and purpose to seek therapy, brought joy to my darkest days, and became my reason to keep going when despair threatened to overwhelm me. I am who I am today because of you. Thank you for coming into this world when you did and for always being my light.

To my husband Chris

I wish I could see myself through your eyes. Your constant encouragement and unwavering belief in me gave me the confidence to share this book with the world. Thank you for being that persistent voice that wouldn't let me quit. I love you more than words can express. You've renewed my life and inner world in ways you may never fully know.

THE HEART RESET

Table of Contents

Introduction

Divorce doesn't just break your heart—it shatters your identity, your routines, and your sense of self-worth. But what if I told you that this devastating pain could become the catalyst for creating your best life? This book will teach you how to thrive through heartbreak and come out stronger than ever. The strategies I've developed aren't just theory—I've stress tested them through my divorce and watched them transform the lives of close friends also dealing with heartbreak. Trust me, if this process could take us from rock bottom to restored, it can work for you, too.

Let me start by saying welcome! Welcome back to the world of dating and single life. You may not want to be here, but here we are. Not so long ago, I found myself in your shoes, unwillingly thrust back into the dating world after my divorce. I was in my late twenties, a new mother to an amazing 9-month-old baby boy, and suddenly facing life as a single mom. Yay? Not quite.

At my lowest point, not only was I coping with new motherhood and financial instability (oh, and full-time business school), but also my soon-to-be ex-husband's years of infidelity, which was forcing me to confront an emotional foundation built on avoidance. As a former NSA intelligence analyst who went from homeless youth to fluent Chinese linguist and Afghanistan combat veteran, I was no stranger to challenging transformations. But untreated PTSD had left me building a life on shaky ground and healing from heartbreak meant first facing the trauma I'd been avoiding. On my journey, I discovered effective strategies that transform heartbreak into profound personal growth.

IMPORTANT NOTE: PTSD is a mind-bender and something a lot of people suffer from, usually undiagnosed. If you think you might have PTSD, or even if you're not sure but have experienced some trauma in your life, I cannot stress this enough: seek professional, therapeutic help NOW, not later.

But this book isn't about PTSD or the poor decisions we make from a place of low self-worth. It's not about why people cheat or even how to survive as a single mother. This book is your practical guide to taking the worst life can throw at you and transforming that pain into power. Drawing from my military background in intelligence analysis, I've broken down the years I spent in the trenches of heartbreak into six clear, actionable steps. Through these six steps, you'll learn how to:

- Understand and move through the stages of grief
- Use therapy as a powerful tool for transformation
- Build daily habits that strengthen your emotional resilience
- Rediscover and intentionally design your identity
- Get crystal clear about what you truly want out of life and love
- Date with confidence and build extraordinary relationships

This book guides you through the day-to-day suffering that comes with abandonment and heartbreak, helping you transform painful moments into stepping stones for growth. I offer you the exact tools that took me from complete despair—dealing with PTSD, single motherhood, and divorce—to creating a life better than I'd imagined possible in just three years.

I was inspired to write this book after close friends who witnessed my journey started asking me for advice on their relationships, breakups, and divorces. As I saw the practices I used to transform my life also working for them, I realized I had tools too valuable to keep to myself. These battle-tested methods have helped real women train their minds, bodies, and hearts to not only overcome pain but to find purpose in it. This system will guide you to intentionally choose the relationships and life you want moving forward, rather than letting circumstance choose for you.

While these strategies have proven powerful for me and the women I've guided, I can only share from our lived experiences. That means you don't have to use every tool or suggestion offered—use what resonates with you. Healing is all about experimentation. This book should be one resource of many you turn to through this journey, not a rigid blueprint for how you "should" approach your very personal process of recovery. That's why I've also provided a curated list of additional books, podcasts, and journals in the Resources section—because sometimes you need a whole toolkit to rebuild your life.

Here's the hard truth: waiting to start this deep inner work only prolongs your pain. Every day you spend stuck in old patterns is a day you could be building the foundation for your best life. This work isn't just about surviving heartbreak—it's about using this breaking point as your breakthrough moment.

I've created the guide I desperately needed during my own divorce—one that addresses the holistic nature of processing heartbreak and rebuilding life after devastation. But there is no one correct answer; no one size fits all. I am giving you my roadmap, but you can choose which paths to take. May this book endow you with what you need and what you didn't know you needed, and may you never again be left in self-doubt or fear.

- CHAPTER 01 -

Understanding Grief

Familiar pain feels safer than an uncertain future, but healing begins when we face the unknown.

If you've picked up this book, you're probably in one of life's most painful transitions: the end of a relationship. Maybe you're newly separated, going through a divorce, or still trying to heal from a breakup that happened months ago. Whatever brought you here, I want you to know something: That pain you're feeling? It's grief—real, legitimate grief. And understanding how grief affects you is the first step to moving through it.

In this chapter, we'll explore:
- *Why breakups trigger grief*
- *The stages of grief*
- *How to recognize where you are in the process*
- *What to expect as you move forward*

The Reality of Relationship Grief

The death of a relationship is like losing someone you love (even if the a-hole is still walking around). Practically speaking, your former partner, the husband you had, is dead to you. And the relationship itself, and the trust associated with it, are, at the very least, forever changed. I want to validate the genuine and intense pain your breakup may be causing you. In addition, understanding the process you're going through can help make it seem less vague, scary, and unpredictable.

The Stages of Grief: D.A.B.D.A.

D.A.B.D.A. stands for Denial, Anger, Bargaining, Depression, and Acceptance—stages originally developed by Elisabeth Kubler-Ross in her work with terminally ill children. People experience these stages while grieving many different forms of loss, including the end of a relationship. If you're unfamiliar with this acronym, you are exactly where I was at the end of my marriage. I hate to break it to you, but the process of recovering from a breakup involves cycling through the stages of grief, as one does with any devastating loss. How encouraging, right? It's not exactly a silver lining associating the end of your relationship with death but stick with me.

I am not your grief counselor or your therapist. Everything I have learned about the relationship grief process has come from my own lived experience, been aided by the professional care of a counselor, and been passed on to friends in need. If you want to gain more in-depth knowledge of grief and D.A.B.D.A., many online resources exist. For this book's purposes, I will break down the stages of grief into understandable and relevant examples to aid you through and prepare you for the overall course of this divorce recovery process.

Before we dive into each stage, there's something crucial you need to understand about grief's nature.

The First Thing To Know About Grief

Grief is not linear. Before I break down this acronym for you, accept this truth: just because the stages of grief are written in a particular order doesn't mean that is the order in which you will experience them. Not only can you jump around, but these steps are also not finite. You may find yourself in one stage of the grief process for a while, then move on to another, and then a month later, to your surprise, find yourself back where you were before. There's nothing wrong with this. It doesn't mean you've backslid or all your hard work is undone. Cycling back to earlier stages of grief simply means you are in grief's very natural, fluctuating, and circular experience, exactly where you should be. As you become familiar with these stages of grief, show yourself grace and empathy because you will experience them all many times in waves. You may feel overwhelmed at first, but in time, each stage will be softer and less frequent.

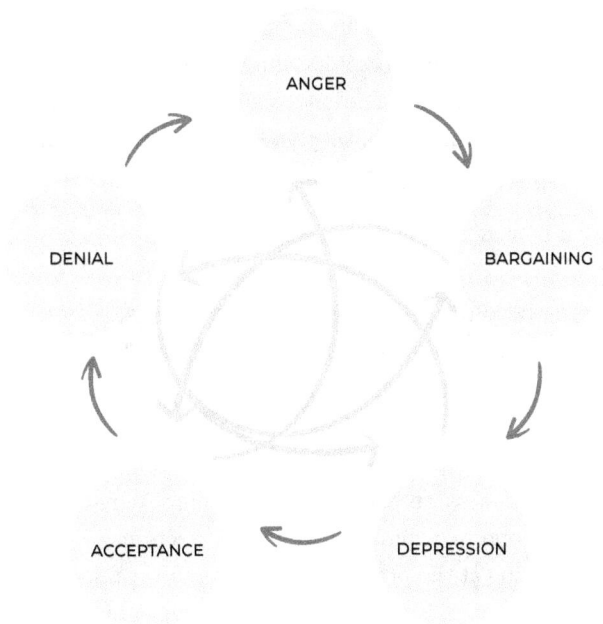

The Experience of Grief

KEY INSIGHTS: Let It Be

- *There's no "right" order to experience grief's stages.*
- *You might revisit stages multiple times.*
- *This process is normal and a healthy part of healing.*

Let's explore each stage, starting with the one that often keeps us stuck the longest.

Denial

Let's just get the cliche out of the way. No, denial is not just a river in Egypt. Refusal to face reality is real, and the desire to keep our heads buried in the sand is powerful. Denial often manifests as an excuse to stay in an unhealthy relationship, driven by the fear of the unknown. Many people can spend years in this phase of grief, remaining in a relationship that has long passed its expiration date. Recognizing this common tendency can help you confront reality and take steps forward. Familiar pain feels safer than an uncertain future, but healing begins when we face the unknown.

Denial Can Look Something Like This:

- I'm better off in this crappy relationship than single.
- My relationship isn't *that* bad. At least he doesn't beat me.
- If my mom put up with that, I can put up with this.

Denial looks like excuses. Even if they are often compelling excuses, they are nonetheless an excuse for something. Why do we make excuses? For one, we think our denial protects us, and in some ways, not looking at the problem squarely in the eye does shield us from facing our pain. However, we assume our denial protects us from something far worse than our current situation. Our denial convinces us that what may come after we leave the cheating husband, the abusive boyfriend, or the addicted father will be worse than the pain we are already familiar with. Familiar is the keyword in that sentence.

The truth is, the only thing scarier to a human brain than continuing to endure the hardship you're already choosing is an entirely unknown, alternative path. This subconscious desire to stick with what's familiar keeps us returning to that toxic or abusive partner. Fear of not knowing what to expect if you finally choose to put yourself out there again keeps you stuck at home waiting and wishing he would call. Denial will keep you in the past, in the circumstance you know, no matter how painful it is—because

to the brain, familiar pain is preferable to an unknown future.

Awareness of your brain's preference for familiar pain and under-standing why this protective mechanism operates so intensely can help you face the unknown future you are heading toward with less fear. Trust yourself. Trust your decision to protect and preserve your heart; you will be rewarded for it.

DIVE DEEPER: Breaking the Comfort of Familiar Pain

1. *What or who am I making excuses for?*

2. *What unknown future am I afraid of?*

3. *What familiar pain am I choosing over the uncertainty of change?*

Moving forward with the awareness of how denial keeps us stuck, let's look at an emotion that, when appropriately understood, can fuel healing.

Anger

I went through this stage many times, experiencing anger, rage, and even murderous rage. Although just one part of grieving, anger remains a common thread throughout the process. We can even become so acclimated to feeling anger regularly at someone else or ourselves that we stop noticing it. However, this unawareness doesn't mean that our fury has gone away or isn't still trying to tell us something.

Anger is necessary, like any other emotion, and has a purpose. Your rage signals that you are a human like the rest of us, not immune to the kaleidoscope of emotion experienced here on earth. Consider your anger a signal that whatever you are grieving now was, at one point, something you genuinely loved and wanted to protect.

> **Anger proclaims how much you cared, even if you want to deny how deeply you've been hurt.**

Acknowledging the information contained in our anger helps us to understand our emotional depth and investment and begin to heal. Anger is a natural response, signaling that you genuinely valued what was lost, and there is no shame in that. Feel it, recognize it, and let it guide your healing process.

Turning anger on its head in this way can be beneficial. Rather than reject our rage, judge ourselves "for still caring" or "not having it under control," ask yourself, would you limit the amount of love you are allowed to feel in order to avoid the possibility of feeling pain? More than likely, the honest answer is no. Your anger just wants to be felt and acknowledged. Anger is a signpost that we have a whole functioning heart that can love deeply and can also hurt deeply. You cannot have one without the other.

DIVE DEEPER: Working with Your Anger

1. What is your anger trying to tell you?

2. What did you love about your partner that you're now grieving?

3. How can you honor this emotion without letting it consume you?

Bargaining

Just when you think you're done with denial, its creative cousin comes knocking: Ah, bargaining, arguably one of the most mischievous aspects of grieving the end of a relationship. Bargaining happens when our excuses for staying in a crap situation turn into desperate strategies or ideas. Here, I will share a personal example with you; my experience shows how uncovering what you truly want can break this cycle of destructive cleverness:

REAL TALK: My *Bargaining* Story

Divorcing my ex-husband was a long road, like death by a thousand cuts. There were days falling down a flight of stairs seemed preferable to the unrelenting heart-wrenching agony I could not escape. There was no single earth-shattering moment—no walking in on him with some woman in our bed. That would have been straightforward, at least, less mind games. Instead, the truth emerged in a slow, torturous drip. Our marriage started idyllically, as they often do. Then, when I was at my most vulnerable, four months postpartum with our newborn son, I discovered dating apps on his phone. I went from preparing for the best, to bracing for the worst. Marriage counseling followed, where he spent every session lying and covering up the extent of his infidelity. At one point, he even hand-wrote me a "confession" letter—which I later learned was filled with carefully curated half-truths meant to quiet my suspicions. Eventually, tired of waking up each morning dreading the next revelation, I took my nine-month-old son and moved out. While separated, the man I had once called my husband finally admitted to two long-term affairs that, combined, had spanned our entire relationship—from dating through engagement and marriage. There was no part of our time together untainted by his deception and disloyalty. Even while separated and begging to stay married, he was still in contact with one of these women, despite her engagement to another man. I had the gutting experience of receiving a screenshot from her fiancé, where my husband declared to her that she was "the woman he really loves."

After reading all that, you might say to yourself, wow, this guy sounds like a real piece of work. Who in their right mind would even consider taking him back? Well, funny enough, it's me! I did! HELLO, BARGAINING!

Twelve months had passed since I had moved out and filed for divorce. We had tried and failed with marriage counseling more than once, and by that point, we both had moved on to dating other people. Yet, my husband still had not even responded to my petition for divorce and kept claiming he wanted to "make it work." So my broken heart doled out one final rationalization, which went something like this:

"The man I'm married to may always lie to me and sleep with other women. Perhaps if I just accept that and work around it, we could somehow stay together and 'make it work.'"

What would this fantasy reality look like? We would remain married, move back in together, and have an "open marriage" (vomit). But I was SO seriously considering this option that I invited my ex over and talked it out with him. He frequented my place for the following two weeks; we attended outings together and slept together again for the first time in months. It was like a trial run, or more accurately, an out-of-body experience. We took the delusion even further and went over hypotheticals of finances and living arrangements. All the while, he was still claiming he only wanted to be with me; I never lost sight of the fact that this "option" required me to never forget who he really was, and ultimately accept that he would always be unfaithful.

So we played this little bargaining game, and then the truth hit me. I only needed a straightforward question and an honest answer to dismantle the pretending. I simply asked myself, what do I want? Did I want to be married to someone I knew I couldn't trust to tell me the truth about where they were or who they were with? Did I want to share a home and raise a child with someone I couldn't depend on to make safe sex decisions in an affair? The answer was a big fat NO. That's when the lightbulb went on. That is NOT what I want, so why am I even entertaining this scenario?! Let's all say it together now: bargaining. Creative, right?

If you can, don't be like me. Instead, ask yourself that Spice Girls question earlier on: What you want, what you really, really want? (I'll help you clear up the answers to this question later.) An honest look at what you really want will hopefully keep you from spiraling into elaborate mental gymnastics designed to protect your heart from grief rather than free you from pain and get you the future and the love you deserve.

KEY INSIGHTS: Save Your Energy

- *Bargaining often disguises itself as "making it work."*
- *The solution usually lies in asking yourself what you really want.*
- *Creative compromises can't fix fundamental incompatibilities.*

Depression

As bargaining eventually fails us, we find ourselves face-to-face with the rawness of our loss, a hard reality to endure. Depression affects many people today, and you don't have to be suffering from grief to experience it. Depression is a challenging stage and can feel overwhelming. If you are someone who, like me, already suffered from diagnosed, clinical depression before my divorce began, the effect can be compounded.

When depression hit during my divorce, I wasn't just sad—I felt like I was wearing a heavy coat made of lead. Some days, just getting out of bed to take care of my son felt like moving a mountain. And you know what? That's normal.

Depression In Grief Can Look Like:

- Struggling to do basic daily tasks
- Losing interest in things you used to love
- Feeling disconnected from friends and family
- Questioning if you'll ever feel "normal" again
- Wondering if the pain will ever end

Let me share something personal about depression and getting help.

REAL TALK: The Reality of Grief Depression

When my son was born in January 2018, I made a decision that would end up being more crucial than I could have imagined. I chose to start therapy to finally confront the PTSD I'd been avoiding—not just for me, but because I wanted to be the best mom possible for my tiny new human. By some twist of fate, or maybe divine timing, I started counseling that February, just two months before I'd discover the first evidence of my husband's betrayal.

Having my therapist already in my corner when everything started unraveling was a blessing I hadn't known I'd need. See, I'd attempted suicide at 23 and lived—but now, even in my darkest moments of depression during my divorce, my counselor kept reinforcing one vital truth: I had a son to live for. When those familiar thoughts of self-harm crept back in, this steady reminder that my son needed his mother became my anchor to this world. The impact of my therapist's persistent positive reinforcement is exactly why I'm such a fierce advocate for good therapy, and why I've dedicated an entire chapter in this book to helping you find the right therapist—because having that support can literally save your life.

I want you to remember that depression, like any emotion, comes in waves. Having this perspective on it and a solid support system around you, can keep you far enough from despair so when the blanket of depression comes, you can endure. Every stage of this grief process is just that, one stage. They are temporary, and with time, the bad feelings dull. Being reminded of the impermanence of negative feelings or emotions is half the battle in releasing their grip.

Depression will come, and it will go, and it is not "who you are." In the meantime, this book will provide you with powerful tools to support you through the thick of it.

The most important thing to remember about depression is that you don't have to weather it alone. While this book offers tools and understanding, depression during grief can be particularly overwhelming. Don't hesitate to reach out to a mental health professional if you find yourself stuck in this stage or if the waves feel too intense to handle on your own.

Managing Depression:

- Remember: This stage is temporary.
- You are not your depression.
- Help and support are available and sometimes necessary.

Acceptance

Once you've spent time moving through the storm of earlier stages, you'll eventually begin to find yourself approaching what might seem like the promised land—acceptance.

So, we've finally made it to the rainbows and butterflies stage of grief, right? You're ready for the accepting and letting go part. Not so fast. Acceptance sounds a lot easier than it feels. What does it mean to accept the reality of your situation (which, by the way, is the first step in being able to take action to improve it)? Well, you must first stop trying to manipulate or avoid the process of your divorce. Stop waiting or hoping for a different outcome. When we stop hoping to get back together with our exes, we realize:

the only thing we are ever powerful enough to change is ourselves.

Acceptance doesn't just mean accepting that your ex is an a-hole and will always be an a-hole, so you stop trying to change, deny or downplay that. It means you also acknowledge your role in the relationship dynamics. When you achieve real acceptance, you can accept that YOU played some role in your own suffering. That sucks to hear, doesn't it?

Or maybe you were one of the brilliant and emotionally genius ones. You naturally excelled at setting boundaries and never took rejection personally. When you realized the person you loved wasn't actually who they had presented themselves to be, you were able to immediately accept that and make the appropriate adjustments without resistance. (Some would describe this phenomenon as having a "secure" attachment style). But if this is you, chances are you won't be reading this book because you probably already have matters of the heart well-managed.

However, if you are like me and many other women whom I know personally and whose stories I have heard, you must now face a reckoning. Having stayed in that difficult relationship does not make you dumb or weak, and beating yourself up for not leaving sooner serves no purpose. Instead, recognize the deeper truth: life offered you essential lessons about partnership, love, boundaries, and your own worth. You stayed because these lessons needed to take root in your heart and mind.

Acceptance means taking ownership of the partner you chose, the behavior you tolerated, the disrespect you endured, and the excuses you made for your partner at your own expense. This brave acknowledgment of *all* aspects of the circumstances, and the role *everyone* played in them, is the only way to ensure you never repeat it again. Taking this kind of radical ownership is the only way I've found to truly start over. And that is what this book is really about.

Signs of True Acceptance:

- You can acknowledge both your ex's faults and your faults.
- You've stopped trying to deny or escape reality.
- You're ready to learn from the experience.
- You can imagine a better future.

As we wrap up our exploration of grief's terrain, let's pull together the key pieces of this healing puzzle.

Bringing It All Together: Beyond Grief

Through this whole grieving process, the heart is trying to get down to three main things. One is the forgiveness of your partner for however you feel they have harmed you. This kind of forgiveness isn't for them, it's for you. Another is taking responsibility for your role in your own suffering in order to learn and grow and, hopefully, never make the same mistakes again. And lastly, to forgive yourself. Many people find comfort in blaming their ex-partner entirely for their heartbreak. Though this feels more comfortable and society often encourages this view, placing all blame on others strips away your power and blocks your growth. True healing begins when you examine your choices and take responsibility for decisions that were against your best interests. Love yourself enough to acknowledge your role in all relationships because this kind of radical honesty opens the door to genuine change, and you are far more in control than you may feel.

> Honest self-reflection is an act of love, and through this honesty, we unlock our power.

KEY TAKEAWAYS:

1. *Grief is a natural response to relationship loss.*
2. *The grief stages aren't linear – you'll cycle through them.*
3. *Each stage serves a purpose in your healing.*
4. *Understanding the process helps make it less scary.*

As we move forward, remember that healing is not linear and that grace and empathy for yourself are crucial. In the next chapter, "Go To Therapy," we'll delve into why therapy is a powerful tool for recovery and growth. I'll guide you through finding the right therapist and making the most of your sessions. Stay with me as we explore how professional support can be a game-changer in your healing journey, helping you rebuild and reclaim your life.

BEFORE MOVING ON:

1. Which stage of grief do you recognize yourself in right now?

2. What's one thing you learned about grief that brings you comfort?

3. What support do you need as you move through these stages?

- CHAPTER 02 -

Go To Therapy

Nothing is more powerful or valuable than someone who is in control of their thoughts, feelings, and actions.

If you've made it through Chapter One's exploration of grief, you might be thinking, "Okay, I understand what I'm going through, but now what?" That's exactly where therapy comes in.

Do you know who needs a therapist? Everyone. So don't take this one personally. Therapy is essential for personal growth and healing, especially after a breakup. Even if you "feel fine" or "the break up wasn't that bad," please, for the love of growth, go to therapy. I firmly believe that the world would be a better place if every one of us were in treatment.

In this chapter, we'll explore:
- *Why therapy is essential for everyone, not just those in crisis*
- *How to identify and work with unconscious beliefs*
- *What makes a great therapist*
- *Different types of therapeutic treatment and their benefits*
- *How to access therapy, regardless of your situation*

Understanding Our Mental Programming

From a young age, most of us are conditioned to have certain *expectations* about life, how it should be, and how people in our lives "should be." But most of all, we are conditioned to believe there is a way *we* should be.

Now, there isn't necessarily anything wrong with having a belief structure. Having internal rules for living helps us navigate our way through the world, defines our preferences, and allows us to choose friends, careers, and goals. But problems show up when the beliefs in our life, of which we may not even be aware, begin to give us results we don't want. These subtle beliefs can be innocuous; for example, "people who litter are bad." You probably won't think this to yourself consciously every day, but if you see someone you are dating often litter, you may find yourself less drawn to them over time.

But subtle beliefs can be much more insidious and cause us to walk down paths we never consciously chose. Some examples of these subtle beliefs are "I always mess things up," "I'm ugly, so I'm lucky anyone loves me," or the mother of all, "I'm not good enough." These often *subconscious* beliefs about ourselves are implanted somewhere along the lines of life, whether by a well-meaning but critical mother or vicious bully. Like weeds, they burrow into the subconscious, ultimately infecting your relationships with others and yourself.

DIVE DEEPER: Examining Your Beliefs

1. What expectations were you taught about relationships?

2. What "shoulds" are running your life?

3. Which beliefs might be holding you back?

4. What stories about yourself need updating?

Your subconscious beliefs can be responsible for the lousy job you hate but can't seem to quit. They could be the reason the man you love is also the man who's cheated on you multiple times. And they could be responsible for keeping you from the beautiful life you deserve and can most definitely have. Let's look at how therapy helps break these patterns and create new ones.

Therapy is a powerful tool that can help you unearth unconscious and destructive thoughts.

Bringing these destructive thoughts to light is the first step in replacing them with something *constructive*. This process will change your life from the inside out.

So let me repeat this. Go. To. Therapy.

We are lucky we live in a modern age where there is increasingly less stigma attached to focusing on our mental health and seeking therapy treatment. However, I do wish there were less discussion around diagnostic forever labels like "anxiety" or "depression" (which coincidentally turn you into a lifelong pharmaceutical customer) and more emphasis on the *plasticity of mindset*.

You don't need crippling anxiety to see a mental health professional. Nor do you need to be severely depressed or suicidal. In fact, please, *please*, do not wait until you have reached either of these landmarks to get yourself a good therapist. Therapy should be looked at as a mental health maintenance program. In the same way you go to the gym regularly, brush your teeth every day, and tidy your house, you should be strategizing your mental-growth game with someone who has the tools to get your mind in the place you want it to be and to keep it growing.

Why Therapy Now?

- You don't need to be "broken" to benefit
- Prevention is better than repair
- Growth happens in small, consistent steps

Great. Now that we all agree that everyone should be in therapy let me relate this to our overarching theme: heartbreak.

As I said earlier, don't wait for a catastrophe to find a good therapist. But maybe you're already in a crisis, and that's okay. Because you're reading this book, I know you're already into helping yourself and growing. Taking the next best step of finding a therapist will be easy, and I am here to help.

While understanding why therapy matters, let's discuss what makes it work.

Finding Your Perfect Therapy Match

What makes a good therapist?

1. They Validate EVERYTHING You're feeling

And when I say everything, I mean EV-REE-THING. A good therapist validates all your feelings, creating a safe space to express even your darkest thoughts. This validation is crucial for emotional healing. Now, there is one minor caveat to this: if a mental health professional believes you pose a real danger to yourself or someone else, they are required by law to report that. But don't worry, I spent many therapy sessions explaining in detail all the physical pain I wanted my ex-husband to experience, and my therapist understood that didn't mean I would inflict that pain on him in real life. This simple act of expressing *out loud* the depth of your hate and anger, and your accompanying gruesome desires, can help evict these toxic thoughts from your mind for good. And this is where the magic of therapy begins.

If you do nothing else with your therapist besides dump every negative and hateful thought you've ruminated on for the week or two between appointments, you will still be getting ahead! Isn't that amazing? Especially in a world where "good vibes only" is touted on t-shirts and mugs, and "nobody likes a complainer." Your therapy session can be the relief valve to the pressure building in your *unwanted negative thoughts repository* (yes, that is a thing).

Signs Of A Validating Therapist:

- Makes space for all emotions, even the ugly ones
- Doesn't rush you to "get over it"
- Helps you understand why you feel what you feel
- Creates a judgment-free zone of trust

There are other ways to get the unwanted thoughts out that I'll cover later in this book, but I bring up therapy FIRST because it is a *vital* tool in this process. Yes, you can journal on your own and commit to other effective daily habits. Still, at the end of the day, a therapist will hold you accountable to the goals you set for yourself. Even better than that, they serve as record keepers who can, at any moment, remind you of where you started, how far you've come, and how justified you are in your pain.

Good therapy chronicles the fruits of your labor and your healing.

2. They Give You Homework & Goals

What you may start to notice about me as you read this book is that I am an action-oriented person. My commitment to action over analysis paralysis is new and something I've had to train myself in. For the first half of my life, I spent more time in my head, lost in ruminating thoughts, than actually out in the world taking steps toward what I wanted. Many of us, especially women, get caught up in our thoughts and never make it to action. So let me tell you right now: this book won't do anything for you if you don't take these tools and actually use them. Just like therapy won't get you the results you want unless you turn your sessions from only venting into strategy brainstorms.

I have tried out many therapists on my journey of self-growth, and I can tell you a quick way to spot the best ones. The ones that want to empower and rehabilitate their patients have one thing in common: they set you up with a *goal* and send you home with a *plan*. Effective therapy involves setting goals and receiving homework to work towards them. This approach ensures progress and accountability.

What Good Therapy Homework Looks Like:

- Identifying healthy coping mechanisms to use between sessions
- Setting up a plan for when a triggering situation occurs
- Journaling prompts or reflection exercises
- New behaviors or thoughts to practice

Sounds simple enough, but I cannot tell you how many counselors or therapists I've started with, and then, after a few months, I began asking myself, why am I even here? What are we doing? Do I just come and complain twice a month, or is there more to this? A great therapist will offer more from the beginning.

When you start a treatment plan with a therapist, if they don't ask you what your treatment goals are, tell them you are interested in setting some. If they immediately jump on board, you're probably in good hands. But, if they give you a confused look like, *"Why are you making my job harder than it has to be? Just come in, talk for a bit, then leave, and don't forget to pay on the way out."* Then, RUN!

Without a goal, you can have no strategy, and without a plan, you'll wind up just spending an hour complaining, followed by leaving in a negative state, feeling helpless, and reminded of all your problems with no clue how to fix them.

Here are some examples of goals I have set with my own counselor.

Therapy Goals Examples:

Goal: Reduce negative self-talk
Action Steps:
- *Identify negative thought patterns*
- *Learn to challenge them*
- *Practice new thought*

Goal: Replace destructive coping habits
Action Steps:
- *Identify triggers*
- *Develop realistic response plans*
- *Build healthier alternatives*

Once you have some goals in place, you and your therapist should then work together to start moving toward your goal in a structured way.

Coming up with a strategy to help you respond less reactively to triggers is one possibility for which you can develop a plan. Say you know a person or situation is incredibly triggering for you emotionally. Your therapist can help you formulate a plan of action for the next time you are confronted with the trigger. Knowing what actions to take in advance keeps the brain from relying on pure fight-flight or freeze mode and can save you from bashing your ex's car windows in with a bat or messaging every girl he's been on a date with since you broke up to tell them how awful he is. Wouldn't it be great to know you have someone in your corner (i.e., a therapist) who can help you navigate these tricky emotional challenges? Yes!

There are any number of strategies your therapist can recommend to you based on your personal goals in treatment. With these aspects covered and a great therapist on your team cheering you on and keeping track of your wins, there is no way you can fail at putting your heart and maybe even your life back together.

Making Therapy Work For You: The Practical Stuff

I'm sure for many of you, your first line of resistance to therapy is the cost, and rightfully so. I don't live under the delusion that every person can afford to see a professional therapist on a regular schedule, nor that they have health insurance that will cover the cost. However, I stand firmly behind my belief that if you can afford therapy, you *must*, even if you have to give up some other discretionary expenses. Nowadays, thanks to technology, there are innovative ways to get mental health treatment that meets you where you're at. There is online counseling through websites like

PlushCare. Therapy can be expensive, but if you are low-income, there are affordable options like community crisis centers. At any income, investing in your mental health is worth it. And if you scour for affordable options but still cannot find the money in your budget, then I'm sorry to say, you're still not off the hook.

Excuses are self abuses. - Yogi Bhajan

You can take your mental health and your emotions as seriously or unseriously as you'd like. But using excuses to avoid these subjects will only prolong and increase your pain. I say this because I know most of you reading this book *can* afford some type of treatment and are capable, at the very least, of seeking out aid that can help you pay for therapy, whether through friends, family, or social and public programs. Online support groups and forums are also great low-budget places to start.

For most of us, taking the time for growth is a choice within our ability to make. And doing nothing is also a choice with its own consequences, like it or not. Either you choose to improve your life or let it continue on its downward spiral. And if you can only afford the bare minimum, there are several books you can read on effective therapeutic strategies and processes. All are free to borrow from the public library. You can find my reading suggestions at the back of this book.

Accessing Therapy:

- Traditional in-person therapy
- Online platforms like PlushCare
- Support groups and forums
- Sliding scale clinics
- Insurance-covered options
- Public health resources

Types of Therapy: Finding Your Fit

In this last section, I want to share a few types of therapy I am familiar with, have experienced, and have benefited from. I've included one type that you can do for free on your own or with the help of a therapist. Two others are typically done with the guidance of a professional trained specifically in that form of treatment.

1. Thought Work (CBT): FREE!

What It Is:

- Cognitive Behavioral Therapy
- Changes negative thought patterns
- Self-guided option available

Cognitive Behavioral Therapy (CBT) helps you intercept and change negative thought patterns. I'm so grateful I stumbled upon CBT early on in my divorce. When I first discovered this thing called "thought work," taught by master certified life coach Kara Loewentheil in her podcast *Unf*ck Your Brain*, I had no idea I was building *cognitive-behavioral models*. I didn't know what *cognitive behavioral therapy* was, nor had I been to a therapist who practiced it. I did, however, understand the concept that my thoughts caused my feelings and that my feelings drove my actions. And this process was responsible for the results of my life. I also fell in love with the idea that simply by becoming aware of the negative thoughts behind my negative feelings and actions, I could replace them with conscious positive ones of my choosing! I was changing my thoughts and changing my emotions all at the same time. This process not only improved my daily levels of happiness but also improved how I interacted with the people in my life who I had been fiery and contentious with for so long. As a result, my anxiety levels were lower. My hope for the future was higher.

REAL TALK: From Rock Bottom to Revelation

I still have a vivid memory of one night during my divorce. My son was at his dad's—we shared custody—and I was alone in my little duplex, crumbling under the weight of self-pity and despair. One thought kept circling in my head like a vulture: "I wish things were different." I hated my circumstances. I hated that I had unknowingly married a serial cheater. Though I was deeply grateful for my son and drew strength from him, I hated the fact that I'd be sharing custody for the next 18 years with someone who had hurt me, discarded me, and carelessly destroyed our family. I hated that he wouldn't change, no matter what I did. I was essentially forced into this divorce because every alternative was worse—and I just couldn't accept that.

There I was on the bathroom floor, sobbing—and I mean really sobbing—from my core. My duplex shared a thin wall with my neighbor—the kind that usually made me muffle my tears—but that night, my self-consciousness vanished as gut-busting wails erupted from somewhere deep inside me. I was at bottom. I couldn't go lower; lower would have meant returning to those dark places of self-harm and suicide. But now that I was a mom, that wasn't an option.

What was an option was choosing a new thought.

When the guttural forces bubbling up from inside me finally ran dry, I picked myself up and reached for my journal. What did I want to feel? It certainly wasn't utter hopelessness, regret, and despair. First, I wanted to stop wishing things were different—to stop resisting a past I couldn't change. So, I shifted my focus from the unchangeable past to the unwritten future. I became awakened to the new opportunity this gut-wrenching end was ushering in, whether I was ready for it or not. A new future? That was something I could get on board with. I let my mind run wild. Yes, what happened was painful and awful, and maybe I wasn't ready to fully accept it and let go, but I was ready to ask new questions: What do I want moving forward?

I knew it wasn't this! Hence the divorce. I wanted a life partner who valued and cherished me, our relationship, and our family. That possibility only existed in my future, not in my past and not with my ex. What I had done here was weave a new option into my tapestry of believable thoughts. Maybe, just maybe, I could appreciate that this divorce, this ending, was opening the door to a new reality—one where I could be with someone who doesn't continually lie. I knew I not only deserved that, but my son did too. This new optional thought became my little glimmer of light whenever I felt myself falling back into that pit of despair. Yes, I wished things were different, BUT I could also be glad I was getting divorced because I deserved to be with someone who doesn't continually lie to me.

This powerful shift in focus didn't just create a different feeling in my body—it created a different lived experience as I moved through the healing process and became my testimony to the real power of thought work in action.

Understanding Thought Models:

Here is an example of the above thought model I recorded in my journal. You can see how the thought flows from a particular circumstance and then creates a feeling, which compels action and provides the result. Taking your cognitive behavioral model from unconscious to conscious, or unintentional to intentional, will allow you to be in control of your outcomes rather than a victim to them.

The Unintentional Model: The Old Thought Pattern

↓ Circumstance (Facts/Neutral):	I am getting divorced.
↓ Thought:	I wish things were different
↓ Feeling:	Despair
↓ Action:	Cry
↓ Result:	Ruminate on things I can't change.

The Intentional Model: The New Thought Pattern

↓ Circumstance (Facts/Neutral):	I am getting divorced.
↓ Thought:	I'm glad I'm getting divorced because I deserve to be with someone who doesn't continually lie to me.
↓ Feeling:	Empowered
↓ Action:	Look forward to my divorce
↓ Result:	Feel grateful to finally know the truth about my ex and look forward to finding a better partner.

Keys To A Good Thought Model:

- Separate feelings from circumstances
- One feeling per model
- Distinguish between actions and results
- Find authentic, *believable* new thoughts

Though we often do not feel that our circumstances are neutral, fact-based events, we must momentarily suspend this belief to extract emotional storytelling from reality. Whatever your circumstance is, try to keep the feelings part of it in the feelings section. A circumstance IS a neutral, fact-based event, something a stranger could observe and describe from the outside looking in. Example: "She fell off a chair," not, "she is clumsy and wasn't paying attention like always and fell off a chair." "He yelled at me," not, "I always let myself be bullied and never stand up for myself so of course I got yelled at." We are not trying to downplay anything here, we are trying to bring organization and order to our experiences so we can take control of how we navigate them.

After identifying your neutral circumstance, note either the strongest or the first feeling that comes up. If there are multiple, you may create more than one thought model. But one feeling for one model is where we start. Pay attention to the thought running through your head when you experience this feeling. Sometimes we notice the thought first, sometimes the feeling; this process is personal, but you will need both for your model.

When it comes to the final sections, Actions and Results, you may feel these two are the same thing, but let me explain the difference. The Action is your immediate short-term response to the thought and feeling you just identified. These reactions can range from escaping into a bottle of wine and a Netflix binge to punching a wall. The Result is the repeated long-term effect this thought-feeling-action cycle is having on your life; for example, developing an alcohol problem, not having time to do household chores, or injuring yourself. More often than not, when left unchallenged, an unintentional model creates more of the same negative emotions we don't want. It becomes a self-fulfilling cycle, which is why intervening and inserting new, optional, intentional beliefs is so important and required if you want to change the results you've been getting.

Now for the truly transformative part. Once you have a solid understanding of the unintentional model or pattern you want to change, the next step is to design an *effective* intentional model. The keyword being effective. Your circumstance in the new model does not change, it is still neutral. However, you now get to decide one of two things. How do you want to feel in this circumstance? Or, what is the new result you want to have when confronted with this circumstance? We are not talking about delusion here, nor the toxic positivity that usually winds us up in denial. The key to your intentional model is finding that little whisper of a thought you can actually believe and that inspires the feeling you desire to have in an authentic and unforced manner. You might have to do some digging (perhaps through journaling) to find that thought. And sometimes, we have to start small. Instead of "I am a strong and powerful woman," if that's still too big of a jump and not fully believable in your body, you can start with "I know I could be a strong and powerful woman" or "doing this makes me stronger." With time and practice:

belief in possibility will transform into embodiment

because your new intentional feelings, actions and results will lead you there.

Your First Thought Model:

- Notice your thoughts
- Reframe negative patterns
- Create new intentional thoughts
- Use reminders (like sticky notes) to reinforce
- Track your progress

The Unintentional Model: The Old Thought Pattern

↓ Circumstance
↓ (Facts/Neutral):

↓ Thought:

↓ Feeling:

↓ Action:

↓ Result:

The Intentional Model: The New Thought Pattern

Circumstance
(Facts/Neutral):
Does not change

2. Then
Thought: What new thought will
create that new feeling or result?

1a.Start Here
Feeling: How do you want to feel
instead?

3. Finally
Action: Take notice of what
changed here

1b. Or Start Here
Result: What different result
would you rather have?

This practice of modeling your thoughts, feelings, and actions and choosing new conscious thoughts every day, though you can do it independently, is a GRIND. It involves becoming and staying very aware of the thoughts running through your head and being vigilant at replacing an old negative perspective with a new, positive, believable one every time it pops up. It also requires you to acknowledge that every thought running through your head is in fact *optional*, and you have the right and responsibility to scrutinize these little intruders before allowing them to take root in your mind. There is no way to be perfect at this (or anything for that matter). Still, mood, reactiveness, and emotional resilience improve when you stay committed to this process of conscious thought practice every day. For me, this looked like reinforcing the new thoughts I wanted to implant into my subconscious using sticky notes around my house. I also journaled daily to purge the negative thoughts ruminating in my brain. Through this persistence, I learned to accept that although I couldn't control my ex-husband or his actions, what I *could* control was my reaction to him.

On the other side of this grind is freedom—freedom from the fear of your own mind, self-doubt, and regret for your actions or words. Over time, you will feel secure enough to know that no matter what is thrown at you next, you get to choose how you think and feel about it and how you react to it. Nothing is more powerful or valuable than someone who is in control of their thoughts, feelings, and actions. I have listed more resources on thought work in the back of the book.

2. EMDR: Brain Hacking

EMDR, which stands for eye movement desensitization and reprocessing, is a form of therapy that is lesser-known but extremely powerful at helping you heal from past traumatic experiences. EMDR assists in processing trauma through guided eye movements. The idea for EMDR came from a scientist who noticed that her mood improved every time she walked outside (yay, walking! I will say more about this later). She decided to study this phenomenon and learned that her eyes' movement from one side of the trail to the other, scanning back and forth, was making her feel less upset. Why this happens is pretty sciency, so I'll spare you the minute details. Ultimately, she developed a protocol where people discuss and process traumatic memories while moving their eyes rhythmically from side to side, and remarkably, this simple practice helps loosen trauma's powerful grip. This protocol is now practiced by EMDR specialists whose treatments have led to powerful healing from PTSD. EMDR sessions are fascinating to watch. I suggest you watch a YouTube video on EMDR to understand better how the process works. I will also provide the resource I read on this subject in the back of the book so you can research it more if this sounds like something you could benefit from.

EMDR can help you access and reprocess, so, essentially uncover and put to rest those traumatic events from your past that have been interfering with your daily happiness and/or your relationships. There are less intense derivatives of EMDR that you can do on your own that don't involve paying a therapist. I suggest you try these out! A good time to do that is when you start adding *intentional time alone* to your routine (this is also covered later in the book). The first thing you can do, I already mentioned. Go for a walk! Not on a treadmill, you won't get the benefits of having your eyes track back and forth. Go for a walk outside for at least ten minutes. And if you really want to get into it, maybe leave your headphones behind. Set an intention for your walk, like working through a specific challenge in your life. Allow your mind to relax as you walk, allowing any thoughts on the subject to rise. The thoughts may seem negative, depressing, or even irrelevant, but just let them pop into your head, notice them, and let them go. You may be surprised to realize that when you ask your brain for the answer to a question within this context, it will provide you with one fairly quickly and effortlessly.

Another alternative brain-hacking activity you can give a try is mentioned by Dr. Julie Lopez in her book on EMDR entitled *Live Empowered!* and is centered around creating. First, choose your preferred mode of creating or expressing your emotion, typically through an image made by painting, drawing, collaging, or whatever creative expression you like. You could express yourself through dancing or melody if you are a more physical or musical person. Once you choose your mode, you then—as you create—want to bring up a traumatic event from your past that is still a problem for you. Maybe your father used to hit you every time he drank, and now you can't date any man who drinks even casually—something like this. When you have a traumatic memory in mind, create! Aim to put whatever you think or feel about that traumatic experience into your creation. That can mean splattered paint, ripped paper, or who knows, maybe even setting something on fire. Or maybe don't do that, but you get the idea. The more you engage in this activity, the more you benefit. The act of expressing your internal feelings externally is a small way to begin reprocessing and reducing the hold the trauma from your past has on you.

If you can confront something, you can heal from it,

DIY EMDR-Inspired Practices:

- Mindful walking without headphones
- Intentional creative expression
- Processing through movement

3. Exposure Therapy: Facing Your Fears to Reduce Their Power Over You

This last option is possibly the most uncomfortable, and I wouldn't recommend it for anyone new to therapy, faint of heart, or working with a therapist you haven't yet established a lot of trust with. I say that because the one time I was confronted with this option (regarding a sexual assault I experienced) I was with a therapist I had just started treatment with after moving to a new state. And when she brought it up, I understood the idea behind it. I just, however, was not at the level of comfort with her I needed to dive into something that intense.

Exposure therapy is what it sounds like. If you have experienced a trauma that is still triggering for you in some way, it is common to want to avoid those triggers and avoid dealing with the traumatic experience. However, exposure therapy says you must do the exact opposite to heal and move on from that trauma. You need to expose yourself, in a healthy and safe way, and in a controlled environment, to the precise experience your conscious brain wants to avoid. Though this may seem crazy and painful, even torturous, the idea is that once you walk through the fire, the painful experience will no longer haunt you. The more you expose yourself to what you (consciously or unconsciously) want to avoid, the less power the trauma will have over you. You will learn to cope with the past in healthy and productive ways rather than run from it. Avoiding one's past results in limiting actions and beliefs. Avoiding trauma, while it might seem like the safest option, can trap you. Confronting it or exposing yourself to the pain point to fully process and cope with it can set you free. This process can allow you to fully step into a healthy future relationship unhindered by triggers from past traumatic relationship experiences.

Important Note:

- Not for beginners
- Requires established trust with therapist
- Must be done in a controlled environment
- Only with proper professional guidance

Bringing It All Together: Making The Choice To Grow

Therapy can feel like a big step. Maybe you're still thinking, "Do I really need this?" or "Can't I just figure it out on my own?" I've been there. But here's what I learned the hard way: You can stay stuck in your patterns, recycling the same pain and creating the same results, or you can get help breaking free. Therapy isn't about being broken; it's about being brave enough to look at your mess and say, "I deserve better than this." Therapy is a vital tool in your journey toward healing and growth. Whether you choose traditional therapy, try CBT on your own, or explore EMDR, just start somewhere. And start now. Remember, therapy isn't just for those in crisis; it's a proactive approach to maintaining (or building) your emotional well-being. Every tool I've shared in this chapter, from thought work to exposure therapy, is something I've used to rebuild my life after my divorce.

None of it was comfortable. All of it was worth it.

On the other side of discomfort is a version of you who knows her worth, trusts her gut, and doesn't settle for less than she deserves. This investment in yourself is invaluable. By engaging in therapy, you empower yourself to confront past traumas, reshape negative thought patterns, and ultimately build a healthier, more fulfilling life.

KEY TAKEAWAYS:

1. Therapy is a vital tool for growth, not just crisis management.
2. Working with a skilled therapist provides both validation and accountability for change.
3. Different therapy approaches serve different needs – find what works for you.
4. Regular therapeutic support plus daily practice creates lasting transformation.

In the next chapter, "Powerful Habits," we'll build on this foundation by creating daily practices that support your healing and growth. Therapy is powerful, but what you do between sessions is what really transforms your life. Stay with me as we develop the habits that will keep you moving forward, one day at a time, and bring you closer to the life you deserve.

BEFORE MOVING ON:

1. What are some therapy options in your area?

2. Create one intentional thought model this week and practice your new thought.

3. Write down your therapy goals, even if you're not ready to book that first session yet.

- CHAPTER 03 -

Powerful Habits

Easy to do and easy NOT to do.

Now that you understand the stages of grief and have (I hope) started looking into therapy, it's time to build your daily foundation for healing.

When I was in the depths of my divorce, my Counselor and I came up with what sometimes felt like an impossible prescription for healing. Here's how that conversation went:

Me (dripping with sarcasm): "Good thing I only have to meditate for thirty minutes every single day, journal, write daily gratitudes, and walk outside three times a week just to keep myself sane."

My Counselor (sensing my sarcasm): "What's the alternative?"

That simple question stopped me in my tracks. I knew what my alternative had been for too many years: a one-way ticket into a downward spiral in the form of repeated impulsive and self-destructive behaviors such as drinking too much most nights, having casual and often drunk, meaningless sex, putting myself in dangerous situations, and overspending on things I didn't need. *You can insert your own list of impulsive, self-destructive behaviors here.*

The truth is that creating new habits isn't just about self-improvement; it's about survival. When dealing with heartbreak, having a solid daily routine keeps you from spinning out into that cycle of Netflix binges, wine bottles, and questionable 2 a.m. texts to your ex.

I'm sure you've heard some form of the saying that it's insanity to do the same thing repeatedly and expect different results. And if you're reading this book with the desire to improve the results you've gotten thus far in love, I'm willing to guess there are other parts of your life or daily habits that have room for improvement. Welcome to the club!

In this chapter, we'll explore:
- *Gratitude Practice: A daily ritual to shift your perspective and build emotional resilience*
- *Intentional Walking: 10 minutes outside can rewire your brain*
- *Morning Pages: Your tool for uncovering truth and processing emotions*

In this chapter, we will cover the little things you can add to your everyday routine that, with consistency over time, will improve your emotional resilience and instill in you a growth mindset (if you don't already have one). The habits I will teach you are only a few examples of what I found worked for me that I was able to stick with consistently for an extended period of time. They are also the simplest habits I've gained the most return from.

If you want more in-depth knowledge on why these habits work or more inspiring ideas, I highly recommend the book The *Slight Edge* by Jeff Olson.

Important Note About Change:

Why do I only recommend three habits? Because change is hard. We humans often like to overlook this fact, imagining crash diets and get-rich-quick schemes will transform us. But meaningful change does not come overnight; if it does, chances are it will leave faster than it came. When reading this chapter, I want you to channel the essence of the Tortoise from the classic folk tale The Tortoise and The Hare: Slow and steady. One foot after the other. One day at a time. If taking things slowly means only adding one new habit to your daily routine and working at completing that consistently for at least thirty days before you even consider adding another, GOOD. That actually sounds like a great plan—do that.

Or, go all in. All three at once. And see how quickly you feel overwhelmed. Did I mention these habits are easy to do AND easy not to do?

I'll say it one more time. Go slow. Give yourself space and time to adjust to these new daily changes. Take the time to notice how a new habit changes your day's feeling or pace and affects your mood and relationship with others. Appreciate this slow and steady journey you are on for all its little gifts and little wins. Before you know it, these three habits will come so naturally to you that you'll want more. But first, let's start at the beginning.

Habit One: Gratitude

Some say the vibration of gratitude is the same as the vibration of unconditional love and appreciation—and that it is a vibrational match to the creator of our universe! If that's a little out there for you, no worries. Gratitude also comes highly recommended by every shrink I've ever seen and self-help book I've ever read. It's like a hammer, found in everybody's toolbox. The reason for this is it simply works. But I'm not just talking about gratitude in the general sense, like being a grateful person, although that's good, too. I'm referring to a daily gratitude practice, transcribed (in some form or fashion), to be collected and reflected on.

Daily Gratitude Best Practices:

- What: Write 3 things you are grateful for
- When: Every single day
- How: Journal, notebook, or even social media
- Key: Don't just think it - ink it!

Don't just think about the things for which you're grateful, *write them down.* I highly suggest you write them in a journal. You don't need anything fancy. You could just keep a big piece of paper and a pen on your nightstand, but why not get fancy with it? There are a lot of daily gratitude journals you can buy on the internet. My personal favorite is The Five Minute Journal by Intelligent Change. "Write" can also mean Tweet (I don't know what we're calling tweets now that it's X). I used this method for a while too. Granted, I was tweeting to my following of 0, but the habit stuck.

Making It Stick:

- Set a daily phone alarm as a reminder
- Do it first thing in the morning
- Link it to an existing habit
  (like your morning coffee)
- Find an accountability partner

My best suggestion to make sure you stick to this new daily gratitude practice is to set a daily alarm on your phone that prompts you to write down your grateful thoughts. Or commit to doing it every morning when you first wake up (best option) or every evening before you go to bed. And finally, the BEST way to stick to any new habit is to find someone who can and *will* hold you accountable. You may have a friend who's also reading this book, you can start a gratitude practice with her. Text each other what you're grateful for daily (and watch your intimacy as friends grow). The best part about all these methods is they leave you with an extensive collection of all the fantastic details of your life. Reserves like this can come in handy when life challenges you again.

Leveling Up Your Gratitude:

If you want to leverage the impact of your new daily gratitude practice, add one more step after writing; that step is *feeling*. Purposefully drawing our attention to things we are grateful for prompts our brain to look for evidence of those things throughout our day. Prompt your brain to find evidence for what you tell it, then take the extra second to focus on what you're grateful for and the *feeling* of love, gratitude, or appreciation it creates inside your body. Feeling the literal physical sensations of gratitude improves your ability to call upon those positive emotions or feelings when you need them the most. Think of it like positive emotional muscle memory building. Over time you will improve your ability to hold and go deeper into those positive emotions. It's like a one-two punch. Deliberate positive thoughts equal more consistent positive thoughts, and deliberate positive feelings equal a higher capacity for positive feelings. So write it, then feel it.

Habit Two: The Power of Walking

Walking. Sounds simple enough, doesn't it? Walking is that thing you've been doing since you were a wee babe, as my very Irish grandmother would say. But how could something so simple and every day change your life? As we touched on earlier, one scientist was able to answer that question, which led to the birth of EMDR therapy.

The Science Behind the Steps:

I bring up walking for the benefits of rapid eye movement. Now add to that, while walking outside, you receive:

- Vitamin D from sunlight
- Fresh air for clarity
- Distance gazing that rests your eyes
- Exposure to the natural world

The health benefits of all of these things are undeniably prevalent, and it's the same with walking.

I'm sure you're already waiting for me to give you some guidelines on the type of walking we're talking about here since I didn't hesitate to set boundaries in the previous section. Don't worry. I have inserted all the caveats to these habits to get you *maximum impact for minimum effort.*

Walking Best Practices:

- What: Walk outside (not on a treadmill)
- When: Can be done any time of day
- How: Aim for at least 10 minutes a day
- Key: Set an intention and leave the headphones at home

You already heard me mention Vitamin D, so if you haven't yet guessed, yes, these walks need to be outside. Walking inside on a treadmill is equivalent to just looking at a picture of delicious food instead of actually eating it. With one, you get way more benefits! Eat the actual food, and go for a dang walk outside! Here's the good news. I'm only asking for 10 minutes a day. You can reap all the benefits walking offers in less time than you can take your Thanksgiving dump. Gross, right? Good. I want that analogy to stick with you, so when you don't feel like getting outside for a VERY quick daily walk, you'll think, "It's quicker than a bathroom break," and just go do it.

And that's it. Want to heal or reprogram your brain to see the world in new ways? Want to improve your mood and overall health? Want to do both of those things in less time than you can take a dump? Then do these walks! 10 minutes outside daily. My personal preference is to take my walks in the morning, a serene time to enjoy being outside. But the time that works for you is the time to do it. Happy trails and happy healing.

Habit Three: Morning Pages

Morning pages, first introduced by Julia Cameron in her book *The Artist's Way*, are what they sound like: pages of paper you fill in daily with your uninhibited, free-flowing, and judgment-free thoughts. Notice that "pages" are plural. I don't want you to do one page (obviously, that's not plural). It's not two pages either, but you're getting closer. That's right, you guessed it, THREE. Three whole pages of thought flow, DAILY. Oh, by the way, handwritten. And yes, FULL pages, like notebook-size pages. Not some dinky mini journal pages, Laura; we all know you're busy with kids or whatever, but come on. Do you want change, or do you want another failed relationship that leaves you wondering how you wound up there again? I think we both know the answer to that question.

Morning Pages Best Practices:

- What: Three FULL notebook-size pages
- When: Best done first thing in the morning, when your mind is most open and least fatigued.
- How: Handwritten
- Key: Stream of consciousness (no editing)

> ## To be different, have different, and receive different, we must first do different.

And I'm sure three full daily pages of a handwritten stream of consciousness is drastically different from what you've been doing because otherwise, you wouldn't need this book.

Let me address the skeptics now. You're probably asking, why so specific? Where is she getting this from? Or maybe you're thinking, there's no way this b*tch hand-wrote three pages for 365 days straight. Well, I hate to break it to you, but I did! And yes, it was as challenging as it sounds. BUT the results of this process paid in leaps and bounds. In a year, I went from being completely lost and broken in my divorce, going back and forth with my cheating ex, overdrinking and overthinking, to completely moved the heck on!

So, was it hard? Yes. But the better question to ask here is, was it worth it? And, oh my word, I cannot give you a more resounding yes, yes, YES.

Not Regular Journaling:

Before I heard of morning pages, I knew what journaling was. I had dabbled in it all throughout my life, as any woman or angsty young teenage girl does. But I was never very consistent with it, and whenever I placed my pen down to write, I always felt like I didn't know what to write, or the writing wouldn't be productive if I didn't fully outline the events of my day first or make what I was writing make sense in some sort of cohesive way. In simple terms, I was censoring myself in my journaling practice without realizing it. I was "shoulding" myself out of receiving the benefits of journaling!

Then I read *The Artist's Way* by Julia Cameron. If you are noticing that I am referencing the work and books of others a lot, that's because I AM. When I was going through the uncoupling phase with my ex, I was grasping at straws daily. So when I found any relevant book or podcast to give me some relief from, or hope in, what I was suffering through, I explored it. That is why I'm even able to write this book, reporting the best practices that gave me exactly what I needed in my lowest and loneliest moments.

Finding What Works For You:

When I bring up *The Artist's Way*, I don't want to imply that everyone should read it or work through its process. To be honest, a lot of you would probably hate it. I tried to suggest The Artist's Way to my now Husband in his time of stuckness, and he gave it about three chapters before abandoning it out of sheer disinterest. But then, I know some of you will take note of every book and outside resource I list here because you're like me, and you never know which one will be the key to your awakening. *The Artist's Way* was a key to mine and could undoubtedly be a key to yours. But whether or not you choose to discover that for yourself is not even relevant.

Why The Pages Work:

I am not making up the concept of morning pages willy-nilly just because it worked for me. No, it is the creative professional's method of unlocking the keys to their subconscious. Typically, creatives will do this to find inspiration, and if you experience this positive side effect as well, that is amazing! But these pages offer you something more than a place for inspiration; they offer a refuge from judgment, pain, or shame. Ultimately, the pages reveal the *truth*. You can't take up this daily writing practice and continue to "not notice" how every time your ex feels lonely, he sends you the "what you doing" text. You can't keep making excuses for your sister, who constantly talks about how great your ex was and how she sees him out with a new woman every other week. And you definitely can't go on ignoring that little voice in your heart telling you you're wasting your time and talent in a job you hate. So here it is. You're welcome. The key to your awakening, to your inner knowing.

How To Do Morning Pages:

A final note: They are meant to be a stream of consciousness. That means you put your pen to the paper and don't pick it up until the three pages are complete. If you have to repeatedly write "I don't know what to write" until a new thought pops into your head, then yes, *do that*. The magic happens in the digging! Aside from that, these pages can become whatever you want them to be. And when I say whatever, I mean *whatever*.

REAL TALK: *The Raw Power of The Pages*

Picture this: You storm home after a heated custody exchange with your ex, rage boiling in your veins. In a frenzy, you grab your notebook and fill three pages with an elaborate, Game of Thrones-style torture scenario. Your ex stars as the victim, every gory, castrating detail spelled out in excruciating clarity. If you've reached this point—and I'm definitely not referencing myself here *winks*—then you've grasped the true power of the pages. These pages can absorb the emotions churning inside you like a white-hot knot in your chest, transforming them into cathartic creations and draining their potency from your body. The pages can become the power player in your healing process if you let them. Now, get writing.

Taking Action

When would be a good time to start one, some, or all of these new daily habits? The answer is today—right now. Give yourself this one small step forward today, and then again tomorrow, and again the day after that. Until your little efforts compound into a new version of you, a version you love more deeply, see more clearly and honor with your decisions and relationships.

Your Daily Toolkit:

- Gratitude Practice: 5 minutes to shift your perspective
- Walking: 10 minutes to rewire your brain
- Morning Pages: 30-45 minutes to unlock your truth

These aren't just random tasks—they're your foundation for healing and growth.

Bringing It All Together: Simple Steps, Powerful Change

So now you know what I mean by powerful habits—those small but mighty actions that can change your life from the inside out. Gratitude, walking, and morning pages might seem simple, but they're the tools that build emotional strength and resilience. Remember, change isn't about grand gestures or overnight transformations. It's about showing up for yourself, day after day, even when it feels pointless, or you'd rather stay in bed. Trust me, I've been there.

These habits are compound interest for your soul.

A little investment each day adds up to massive returns over time.

KEY TAKEAWAYS:

1. *Small daily actions compound into life-changing results.*
2. *Consistent habits build emotional resilience and mental strength.*
3. *Starting with even one new habit can transform your healing journey.*
4. *Progress matters more than perfection in building new routines.*

Start small and keep moving forward. Speaking of moving forward, let's get ready for what's in the next chapter, "Rediscover and Transform." We'll explore how life's curveballs can shake up your identity and sometimes challenge everything you thought you knew about yourself. But don't worry, it's not all existential crisis and identity meltdowns. We'll talk about how to use these changes to get to know yourself again and how to shape the person you want to become moving forward with intention. Keep working on those new habits, and let's get ready to face change head-on.

BEFORE MOVING ON:

1. What's one habit you can start TODAY?

2. How can you set up your environment for success (journal by your bed, walking shoes by the door)?

3. Who could be your accountability partner?

- CHAPTER 04 -

Rediscover and Transform

Divorce is not just an ending of one thing but the beginning of a million new, brilliant little things.

In this chapter, we'll explore how divorce or heartbreak can become the catalyst for profound personal transformation. You'll learn that your identity is, in fact, malleable and not predetermined, how to rediscover yourself, and ways to intentionally reshape your social circle to support your metamorphosis. But first, let's talk about something that might surprise you.

In this chapter, we'll explore:
- *Why personality and identity aren't permanently fixed*
- *How to rediscover yourself after significant life changes*
- *The power of intentionally choosing your network*
- *Practical exercises for self-discovery and growth*
- *Tools for assessing and upgrading your social circle*

Understanding Change

Did you know that personality is not permanent? Weird, right? We walk around the world thinking we know who we are and how we would respond in any given circumstance. But until our backs are against the wall, we don't know what our reaction will be. Sometimes, the events we encounter can change what we think to be our most fundamental character traits or behaviors. There are two reasons for this.

The first reason we as individuals can change seemingly so drastically, and sometimes imperceptibly to ourselves, is identity. In social science, an identity is defined as the qualities, beliefs, personality traits, appearance, and/or expressions that characterize a person or group. I would add one word to this definition. That word is "should." Here is the more accurate definition: an identity is the qualities, beliefs, personality traits, appearance, and/or expressions that *should* characterize a person or group. So what does this change do? It inserts our subjective predisposition of what we think *should* characterize a person or group. Our definition of any identity we hold, be it girlfriend, wife, or mother, is entirely based on our unique understanding, belief, or expectation of how we *should* embody that role.

Example: Two women are married to two different men. Both men are cheating on their wives, and both women discover the cheating. The first woman believes a wife does not leave just because her husband cheats. What kind of woman would she be if she got a divorce? Certainly not the wife she was raised to be; she cannot envision her identity as a single mom or divorceé. She stays.

The second woman who discovers her husband's cheating believes that a wife is someone who is cherished, respected, and honored by her partner. If that is a vow her husband would break, then she cannot fully expand into her identity as a wife, nor can she embody the example she feels responsible for setting for her children. She leaves.

Here we have two women with the same identities of wife and mother. Yet they both take opposite actions when confronted with the same circumstance. This difference shows us that your *thoughts* are the main factor determining your personality or behavior in any given situation. Why do these women choose to act differently in the same circumstance? Because these individuals have two different sets of thoughts running through their heads, resulting in different actions. The behavioral difference means that even the same person in the same situation can behave as a fundamentally different person at different times in their life. Such transformation isn't just because the individual has "changed." The transformation occurs because the person's *thoughts* have changed.

My point here is twofold. First, I will prove that who you are is not defined by outside circumstances, or even external identities such as "wife."

> **Who you are is very much malleable and in your control because you are who you choose to be with your thoughts and actions.**

Second, know that any time we realize we don't like who we've "become," we are more empowered when we see that it is well within our ability to improve who we are; all we have to do is choose to improve our *thoughts*. That is what this chapter is all about.

Life, relationships, and especially divorce can pick you up off the ground and shake you around a bit before slamming you back down, leaving you lost and broken. Yet in these moments, there are little floating buoys you can grab onto as you navigate your way back to stasis. I will walk you through the steps you can take and the questions you can begin to ask yourself through this process of self-rediscovery and redefining.

Now that we understand how thoughts shape identity, let's explore practical ways to envision who you are becoming.

1. Rediscovering Yourself

As stated above, the end of a relationship is not simply that. It can also be the end of an identity, the end of yourself as you thought you knew her. Denying the loss of your identity or trying to ignore it does not make it any less impactful. And trying to make yourself fit back into the box you were forcefully ejected from, even with a new person, is futile. You will be different now and moving forward. Congratulations—own it. Let's discuss why this matters so much.

When you move through a cycle of change, picture yourself like the ocean. You are a dynamic vessel, constantly changing and moving in different ways. Your tides rise and fall, and your waters ripple and crash. All the while, this change is affecting so much more than the movement of your tide. It affects everything within the ocean: the sands, the plant life, the fish, the clarity, the salinity. Understanding how globally we are changed can help us lean into this unraveling, dynamically and flexibly. We must embrace that when one aspect of us or our life changes, the rest of who we are may also fall like dominoes, and that's ok. Divorce is not just an ending of one thing but the beginning of a million new, brilliant little things.

God transforms our suffering into gifts multiplied.

Embrace this change and watch this painful ending shift into a tool to redefine your life in a more fulfilling, dazzling, and authentic way. In this chapter, I will guide you through intimate practices you can adopt to seize this beautiful opportunity to rebuild yourself magnificently. The following two chapters are all about intentionally focusing on yourself, your environment, and what you truly desire in order to turn your visions into reality. It's time to level up.

The How

How do you get to know yourself again? Most of us don't spend the time initially thinking about our values, personal mission, or who we are as a person. We are, however, still making these decisions, but we are choosing unconsciously. We adopt our parents' values and our culture's mission, and often, who we are as a person is based on what we think our partner or the world wants us to be. Nothing is inherently wrong with this, but when the core of who you once believed you were has been shaken or even shattered, you need a strategy to clarify what matters most to you *now*.

One of the best ways I know how to do this is by spending time alone. And I don't mean time alone on your couch watching Netflix or scrolling TikTok; I mean quality time with yourself, the same type of time you would want a lover to spend—intimate quality time, focused, loving, and intentional.

Some of the best things you can do for time alone are things that you directly benefit from. I want you to be selfish with your time alone and do something for you, something that will help you get to know this new version of yourself better, such as writing. You can do expressive journaling or write poems, short stories, or narrative nonfiction. You could lay out all your favorite fantasies. You could rework painful or joyful memories more explicitly and intentionally, creating stories based on these experiences. Or you can have a discussion with yourself on paper, asking questions and then answering them from multiple perspectives.

Another great way to spend your time alone is reading. Books or essays may not help you get to know yourself better, but reading can arm you with new tools and ideas to help you expand into the person you're working toward becoming. This book is an excellent example of this, designed to be used as a tool to help you move forward and grow after something painful. There are many great books out there that are super targeted at whatever your specific goal might be. Spending time with these books, and I would suggest at least 10 pages daily, will pay dividends.

Finally, here is a fun exercise you can do relatively quickly to gain a new perspective on yourself and, importantly, the people in your life, which we will dive into next.

EXERCISE: The 5 Traits Mirror

Time needed: 15-20 minutes
Materials: Paper, pen, somewhere to display your results

Steps:

1. Think of someone you know well enough to admire (personal connection preferred)
2. List their top 5 character traits you admire most
3. Write these traits down and post them somewhere visible
4. Finally, congratulate yourself and recognize that you possess these same qualities
5. Practice daily affirmations using these traits

KEY INSIGHTS: Uncover, Believe and Reinforce

- You can only recognize in others what already exists within you
- Affirming positive traits trains your brain to find evidence of them
- What you admire in others reveals your hidden strengths

Wait, what? Yes, that is correct. I remember the first time I was tricked into doing this exercise, wondering where it was going. I did not expect that to be the lesson. But I have discovered it's true. So often, we look at those we admire as this beacon of a person we will only ever aspire to be, but when do we see ourselves as that beacon for others? The answer is now. This is based on the psychology that, in order to perceive another's character trait (this goes for the good and the bad), we must in some way already possess those traits ourselves. We are intimately attuned to those traits *because* we have them. However, what often happens is our own negative self-beliefs, and our self-misperception, gets in the way of seeing that truth.

The person I admired was kind, passionate, joyful, driven, and smart, so the exercise led me to write on a Post-it: "I am kind, passionate, joyful, driven, and smart." Whatever the qualities you write down about the person you admire (and then write down as an affirmation about qualities you already possess), you are empowered to embody because:

Your brain is designed to show you confirmation of what you tell it is true.

Soon enough, your most admirable qualities will become as consciously visible to you as they have already been to others.

The impression others have of us can often seem skewed from how we perceive ourselves. This exercise is a great way to begin seeing ourselves for who and what we truly are. We possess the best qualities we admire in others, even if we don't see them consciously. So, keep this list, tape it up somewhere, and speak it from the perspective of "I am…" every time you look at it.

Once you've started reconnecting with yourself, it's time to examine the people you surround yourself with and how they're influencing your transformation.

2. Transforming Your Network

There's an old saying that if you want to know your future, just look at the lives of the five people with whom you spend the most time. This predictor is more accurate than I'm sure many of us would like to believe. I've witnessed this truth firsthand in my own circle of influence.

One of my closest friends, whom I met during my divorce, was married with two children. Interestingly, we initially bonded over our shared experience with a challenging marriage. The difference was that I had already moved beyond mine, while she remained trapped in a difficult situation that had continued for over fourteen years. Her social circle consisted entirely of highly religious individuals who dismissed her struggles rather than validating them.

As our connection deepened, witnessing my post-divorce transformation began shifting her perspective. This wasn't from any direct advice—I firmly believe only she could determine what was right for her. Rather, seeing my journey toward healing and renewal gave her the courage to eventually advocate for herself in ways she never had before. Now she's embarked on an exciting chapter of self-discovery, learning to embrace independence and champion her needs in both love and life.

I share this story to illustrate how profoundly we're shaped by those around us. My friend had been pressured by her religious parents into marrying someone she barely knew at just 20 years old. She endured this unhappy and sometimes abusive union for fourteen years simply because she'd never seen an alternative path. Many of us remain in unsatisfying circumstances because we're surrounded by others who are *just as stuck*. Breaking this cycle requires intentionally curating your social environment.

Your inner circle can elevate or diminish your life trajectory. Surrounding yourself with inspiring, motivated individuals versus those who constantly complain and embrace victimhood creates dramatically different outcomes.

> **Where you plant yourself ultimately determines how fully you can bloom.**

REAL TALK: Stop Settling

In the early stages of my divorce, I was a new mother to my then 6-month-old son. My ex-husband and I had recently relocated to a new city, where I knew no one but him. I had no family, no friends, and no support system. This was a problem. I needed to make friends fast for any chance at standing on my own two feet. So I took to the internet. I joined many Facebook groups for women in my local area. I even downloaded an app called Peanut to meet other moms, though I never had much luck with that one. Eventually, I found a group of women I thought were great and decided to plant my flag with them. However, I soon learned that these women were not moving in the same direction I envisioned for myself.

They were around my age bracket at the time, mid-to-late 20s. However, none had been married or had kids, nor did these milestones seem close on their horizons. We had a group chat, which I initially liked, but as my time with the group continued, I saw some unfortunate patterns emerging. The chat soon became filled with complaining about men, jobs, lack of money, and general unhappiness with life. The interactions often left me feeling drained and pretty crappy about my future prospects.

Then a question popped into my head: what do I have to gain from this?

That sounds a bit self-interested, and I would argue we should all be self-interested. If you don't look out for your best interests, who else will step in and do so? Taking ownership of my best interests was a turning point in my life. For the first time, I dared to want more for myself, to want better relationships and friends who inspire me and have successes in their lives from which I could learn. For the first time, I realized I didn't just have to humbly accept any circumstance or relationship in which I happened to find myself. I had the power and the responsibility to set standards for myself and my close circle. I chose to distance myself from those caught in a cycle of disempowerment and open space in my life for others who were also seeking a future similar to what I envisioned—or already living that dream. This was transformative.

If your friends are your future, you must assess your network!

EXERCISE: Look Into Your Future

Time needed: 30 minutes
Materials: Paper or journal, Pen, Space to reflect

Steps:

1. List Your Desires (10 minimum)

   - *Include things you have or want to improve and future dreams*
   - *Be specific and honest*
   - *Don't filter or judge what comes up*
   - *Some examples: a loving relationship, financial independence, or your dream body*

2. Map Your Social Circle

   - *3-5 people you spend the most time with or around*
   - *Include people from regular daily/weekly interactions*
   - *Consider family, friends, coworkers*
   - *If unsure, base it on the past week*

3. Now let's throw it back to grade school, Create Your Venn Diagram

   - *Use your List from Step 1 and Social Circle from Step 2*
   - *Right Circle: Your Desires and Goals not (yet) reflected in your social circle*
   - *Middle Section: Overlap between your desires and your social circle's reality*
   - *Left Circle: Current reality of your social circle at conflict with your Goals*

Example

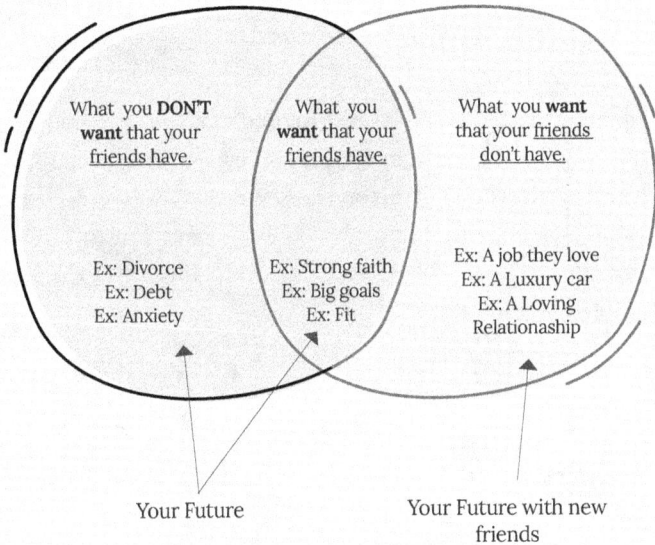

What you **DON'T want** that your friends have.	What you **want** that your friends have.	What you **want** that your friends don't have.
Ex: Divorce Ex: Debt Ex: Anxiety	Ex: Strong faith Ex: Big goals Ex: Fit	Ex: A job they love Ex: A Luxury car Ex: A Loving Relationship

Your Future   Your Future with new friends

4. Reflect & Analyze

- Notice any patterns
- What surprises you?
- Where do you see misalignment?

This exercise will help you become keenly aware of the influences in your life that you may have overlooked before. It should empower you to move more intentionally in the direction you desire. Please make this list at least once a year. Give yourself the challenge to make the far left circle empty! Imagine only being surrounded by those living the manifestations of your desires. Your potential is limitless.

Bringing It All Together: Designing Your Next Chapter

> # Change isn't just inevitable—it's an opportunity for transformation.

Throughout this chapter, we've explored how your personality, identity, and social circle can and should evolve after a significant life shift like divorce or heartbreak. Remember, you're not stuck being who you used to be or who others expect you to be. Your thoughts shape who you become, and you have the power to choose those thoughts intentionally.

KEY TAKEAWAYS:

1. *Your identity isn't fixed – you can consciously choose who you become.*
2. *Time alone helps you rediscover and reconnect with your authentic self.*
3. *Your circle shapes your future – choose your network intentionally.*

In Chapter Five, "Own What You Want," we'll channel all this self-discovery work into something even more powerful: getting crystal clear about what you want moving forward. Not what your ex wanted, not what your parents want, not what society tells you to want—but what YOU truly desire for your life. You'll learn how to identify your genuine desires, create a dream list for your ideal partner, and set boundaries that protect what matters most to you. Stay with me as we transform a shattered heart into a clear vision through radical honesty, conscious desire-setting, and the courage to ask for exactly what you want.

BEFORE MOVING ON:

1. What's one relationship you want to nurture this week?

2. When can you schedule 3 blocks of intentional alone time?

3. Write down your key insights and revelations.

- CHAPTER 05 -

Own What You Want

Why not ask for exactly what you want?

Building on the self-discovery work we did in Chapter 4, now is the time to get honest about what you really want.

Self-discovery takes time and isn't easy; the journey is never-ending. Throughout your life, you will constantly lose sight of and then rediscover or redefine who you are. The tools I gave you in the last chapter are evergreen material to help you do this. No matter your age or the life circumstances you find yourself in, taking time alone to connect to your authentic inner self will always serve you well. Consciously choosing the people in your environment will support you in defining and creating the life you desire. What you want to receive moving forward is our next topic of exploration. What could be more exciting than defining your dreams and making them come true? And the most important step toward achieving your dreams is setting your goals.

We have numerous dreams and desires tied to every aspect of our lives. We have desires related to family, love, wealth, impact, and even legacy. Whether we are consciously aware of what those desires are, though, is another story.

Desires, like any thought, can be either conscious or subconscious. You may be wondering how a desire can be subconscious. Aren't you choosing the things you want? How can you choose something unconsciously? Even more confusing, how can something you don't even realize you're choosing be the very thing that prevents you from having what you actually want? Mind bending, right?

Think of the woman who claims she wants a committed relationship but keeps dating unavailable men because that feels familiar. Her conscious desire conflicts with her subconscious patterns.

Here's the deal: too often in life, we knowingly or unknowingly let go of the wheel and pretend we're no longer in the driver's seat. This practice can come in many forms. For example, a mom may put her dreams on hold for so long that she can barely remember what they were when she finally returns to them. A young woman may graduate college and find herself underemployed in a field she hates, with $90,000 worth of student loan debt and no idea how to figure out what she should be doing instead. Or, a woman who devotes herself to her career may dream every night of the family she never could find the time to start. We all have our own story to tell when it comes to getting lost along the road of life, but it doesn't have to be this way.

Before we dive in, know this: The exercises in this chapter only work if you can suspend your self-judgment long enough to be honest about what you want. Objectivity can be challenging for anyone, myself included. If you feel confused about what I mean, one small way to test if you are being honest with yourself is to assess your feelings about what you discovered throughout this chapter. Suppose you unearth desires that raise some feelings of discomfort, uncertainty, or even embarrassment. In that case, you have most likely entered into truth territory. Conversely, if what you wrote doesn't scare you in any way, you may be camped out in Comfort Land, in which case I'd suggest you take a few more cracks at it.

This chapter is about becoming keenly aware of everything you authentically desire in life and in a partner. Following these steps, you will come to understand how the things you choose every day, consciously or not, determine the quality of your life. By taking the courage to own and reflect on what you have been settling for and what you now want to choose moving forward, you can expect dramatically different results in many areas of your life.

In this chapter, we'll explore:
- *Getting clear on your desires through focused exercises*
- *Understanding what you want in relationships specifically*
- *Setting boundaries to protect your desires and dreams*

Now that we understand how conscious and unconscious desires both shape our choices, and often conflict, let's get specific about what you *really* want.

EXERCISE: *Making The List – Your Life*

Time needed: 5 minutes
Materials: Timer, paper, pen

Make a list of what you want in life. You can add to the list you started in the exercise presented in the last chapter, Look Into Your Future, or you may start anew. I'd like you to set a five-minute timer and go crazy. Don't pick your pen up off the paper until that timer buzzes!

If your life could go in any direction, what would you choose? Be specific and dream big. Pretend you are writing a story, and cast yourself as the main character. Here are some prompts to get you going:

Family & Relationships:
- What kind of family do you want?
- Kids, no kids? Or how many kids?
- Adopted or biological?
- Would you stay home with those kids, or would your partner?
- Describe your ideal partner.

Career & Lifestyle:
- And how would all this complement your career if you choose one?

- Would work and family be beautifully symbiotic, or would they be appropriately compartmentalized?
- Or would you just be a retired millionaire at 35?

Impact & Legacy:
- What impact do you want to have on your children?
- What impact do you want to have on your community or even the world?
- What greater purpose do you feel called to?

Spirituality:
- Do you have a daily meditation practice?
- Maybe you'll find peace in going to church again.
- Who would you like to forgive?
- How do you want to feel when you wake up in the morning? Are you excited for the day or peaceful and content?

As you can see, this exercise is all about imagining your ideal life, including work, family, wealth, and spirituality.

Making this list (and writing it down!) is just one tiny first step in the direction of the life you truly desire and are entitled to consciously choose. Without making a list like this, you may wind up like one of the women in my earlier examples, lost in a situation you never really wanted.

Once you've completed this exercise, you can begin to make an action plan! But what does this look like? Do you just up and change everything in your life? The answer is, you don't have to do a dang thing. You can go on living your life buffeted by the winds of fate, landing wherever you're tossed. But I want you to know you have another choice. You can start making choices that lead you in the direction of the life you created on your dream sheet. You can take drastic action, such as selling your house and moving to Hawaii, or make subtle changes, like asking your partner to turn their phone off an hour before bed to make space for more intimacy in the evening.

Let me share how I put this into practice in my own life.

REAL TALK: No Time for Dating Games

At the end of my divorce, I reconnected with an old flame from years past. It felt like no time had passed since we'd last spoken, and the natural reconnection was undeniable. It wasn't long before we went all in and decided to live together. Deciding to cohabitate was no small step since I shared a 2-year-old with my ex-husband. My new partner and I weren't just testing a relationship; we were creating a potential family.

After my first marriage, I decided that when I finally took this step with someone again, I would be clear from the start about what I desired from the relationship. The biggest mistake I made with my first marriage was letting my partner choose me before deeply knowing what I wanted from the relationship.

This time, I made a point to clarify in my mind and then tell my partner candidly what I wanted for my future. I hadn't given up on having a beautiful family with a strong and supportive life partner. That's why I stopped dating around and chose this person. And I knew I wanted my son to be close in age to any potential siblings, so that meant the family thing had to happen sooner rather than later. Being so upfront about my family planning goals may seem like a huge risk, but I knew my heart's desire and was honest about it. I also knew if I was with the right partner, they would empathize with and support my dream of a family.

So after only a few short months of living together, and with no ring on my finger, I sat my boyfriend down and told him my ideal scenario. I told him I was in a relationship with him because I wanted to connect deeply and build a life and future together, which meant I saw myself having more kids within the next couple of years. I told him if that was not an option for him, we needed to talk about what to do next, because my time was precious.

Going into this conversation, I prepared myself for the worst-case outcome of him not being on board, which would have meant I'd need to start dating again—Bummer. But I knew my own strength and that I could handle anything for the sake of the vision I had for my life. Fortunately, my boyfriend listened to everything I said, and at the end of making my desires known, he said he shared my vision for our future. We started trying for a family that day.

This scenario might not be ideal for every woman. You may think I sound reckless. But I want you to draw two points from my example. First, others will always judge the desires of your heart, but as they are not the ones who have to live your life, they shouldn't get a say in how you live it.

Why not ask for exactly what you want, even if it seems reckless at times?

My second point is that I got exactly what I wanted! I asked and, boom, I got my needs met *immediately*. Was it difficult to finally bring this sensitive subject up in conversation, and was I nervous as hell? Yeah, but it was worth it. We may not always get everything we ask for, but if you never dare to ask in the first place, you may never get anything you want. Instead, you will live the life that either someone else wants for you or that just comes along.

DIVE DEEPER: Having It All

1. What desires did you uncover that surprised you?

2. What is something you deeply want, but have been avoiding asking for?

3. What's the worst thing that could happen if you ask for what you want?

4. What's the best thing that could happen if you ask for what you want?

Be emboldened to fully embrace the life you desire, and feel encouraged to align your actions and communication with your goals. It's time to start being honest with yourself and the people around you about what you truly want.

> **KEY INSIGHTS:** *Choose and Claim*
>
> 1. *Getting clear about your desires is the first step to achieving them.*
> 2. *Being honest about what you want takes courage but is truly freeing.*
> 3. *Taking action, even small steps, is better than staying stuck.*

Now that we've explored your life's desires broadly, let's focus on one specific area that often gets complicated by other people's expectations: romantic relationships.

Part 2: The Relationship of Your Dreams

We just finished going over some strategies to help you get in touch with whatever deep or uncovered desires you have at this new point in your life. If one of those desires involves a loving and supportive relationship, great! Keep reading. If not, that's ok. You can save this section for when you feel ready.

If you are ready then it's now time to...you guessed it...make another list! I remember the first time I received this prompt. I felt weird about creating a description of my dream lover, to say the least. I felt like doing so was wrong, as if making a list of everything I wanted in a partner and expecting it was somehow arrogant or presumptuous. How could I ever find someone who met all my criteria and, even if I did, would I meet their expectations? I felt I was being asked to perform a useless task for an impossible end. So if that's how you feel at first, I get it.

But I don't want you to write this list with the expectation that you will find some perfect man who checks every box (though I hope you do), because this list isn't designed to set you up for disappointment. The purpose is to gain clarity on what your expectations of a great partner even are.

> **When you know the type of partner you want, you will find it much harder to settle for whoever is around when you feel lonely or sad.**

Why not make it easier to avoid another disappointing match? Not only will you be more equipped to filter through incompatibilities, this list will help you honestly communicate to your next partner what exactly your expectations of them in a relationship are when you get to that point. I cannot express how much it will change your life to tell a man exactly what you want. I could write a whole other book about why it's so difficult for some women to ask for what they want and why it's such a mistake to want your partner to know or guess instead.

Expectations

EXERCISE: *Making The List – Your Partner*

Time needed: 15 minutes
Materials: Paper, pen

Now you will make your dream sheet! Avoid adding superficial expectations to your list, such as physical build or pet peeves. Generally, this should be a list of DOs, not DON'Ts, and these should be make or breaks for you, nonnegotiables. Your list should focus on how you would like your partner to treat you and the positive experiences you look forward to sharing with them. These are the things you know you are deserving of in a relationship and should not have to settle without. Here are some examples from my own life.

My Future Husband's Relationship Goals:
- Desires to be in a monogamous long-term relationship
- Is open to growing with me (this is an affirmative version of 'not defensive in arguments')

Connection & Communication With My Future Husband:
- Will want me to feel included with his friends and family
- Can have philosophical conversations just for fun
- Plans dates for us without me asking

My Future Husband's Personal Growth:
- He has his own ambitions
- Inspires and empowers me to chase my dreams

Not everything on your list needs to carry the same weight. Some items might be absolute must-haves, while others could be strong preferences.

Once you've completed your list, you now have the typically unstated list of expectations every man wishes he had on hand when he can't figure out why you're mad at him again. I'm not going to outright tell you to give this list to your current partner or future one when they come along, but I'm also not saying you shouldn't.

When I first did this exercise, I mentioned it to the person I was dating at the time, and he jumped at the opportunity to see it! His interest in my happiness was a beautiful thing to experience. If you meet a man who is so interested in you that he is excited about an opportunity to learn everything you desire from your relationship, that's a man interested in your happiness! When someone loves you, they want to make you happy. Why not make that easier for them with some transparency around your desires and expectations?

On the other hand, you don't have to share this list with a potential partner if you don't want to for whatever reason. You may want to do more trust building first, or are unsure about your own level of interest and commitment. Either way, you will still benefit from knowing what's on your list because

> **clarifying your desires will guide your boundary-setting and ability to confidently and honestly communicate what you want.**

Speaking of boundaries, knowing them AND expressing them is where the rubber meets the road. Clear desires and expectations are great, but boundaries are what *protect* them. Let's talk about what that means.

Boundaries

Before we dive into common myths about boundaries, let's get clear on what a boundary is: it's a guideline you set for yourself about how you'll respond to situations and behavior.

> **Boundaries are not about controlling others; you set boundaries to manage _yourself_.**

Lately, the value of setting healthy boundaries has thankfully been mentioned in mainstream dating culture. However, understanding _how_ and _why_ boundaries are implemented and enforced requires a deeper conversation. Let's walk through the common myths about boundaries found in mainstream culture.

Myth 1: Boundaries are a way to coerce someone into behaving a certain way.

This is a tempting one. It's almost like emotional extortion. You tell your partner that you will enact XYZ if they do ABC again. And that is your "boundary". You are telling them they are not allowed to do that thing again, and you hope that by threatening them with a very dire response from you, you will coax them into being the version of themselves you find most acceptable.

Example: Sarah tells her boyfriend, "If you keep playing video games after 8 p.m., I'll start going out with my friends every night without telling you where I am." She's trying to use a threat to make him change his gaming habits.

Example: Tom tells his girlfriend, "If you don't start dressing more conservatively, I'll start flirting with other women to show you how it feels." He's using a boundary as leverage to control her choices.

Hate to break it to you, but this NEVER works. And if you make the mistake of believing threats will get you what you want, you're setting yourself up for disappointment. You are tricking yourself into thinking your threat will squeeze your partner into being who you want them to be when the reality is people change their behavior when they choose to, generally for reasons that will benefit them.

Lasting change does not come from an ultimatum disguised as a boundary.

What will this type of boundary-setting get you? Either you will be forced to make good on your threat because this kind of boundary will likely not deter their inevitable behavior, which could result in a massive blow-up of whatever relationship you were hoping to salvage. Or you won't make good on your threat and will wind up damaging your credibility with your partner, who now may see you as someone irrational who doesn't stick to her word and can be easily dismissed. Worse, you will damage your credibility with yourself. Not being able to trust yourself to be your biggest advocate and protector can damage many areas of your life.

Reality: True boundaries are about taking responsibility for your responses and actions, not trying to control someone else's.

Example: "When you play video games after 8 p.m., I'll plan other socially fulfilling activities since quality time is important to me."

Myth 2: Boundaries are a way to punish others for unwanted behavior.

This myth has a similar ring to the first, but it's slightly different and worth mentioning. The first myth uses manipulation and coercion to try to change someone else. Though still externally focused, this boundaries-as-punishment myth is more a tool of retribution. You don't want or need to fundamentally change your partner. Still, you feel compelled to punish them for something they did, purposefully or not, in the name of a "boundary," or more accurately, hurt feelings. An example is when your partner says something to you in an argument you don't like, so your "boundary" is to refuse to speak to them for the rest of the day. Giving someone the silent treatment is a way of getting the final word in, so that instead of collaborating on solutions to the problem so you can grow, learn, and move forward, you insist on ending your exchange with the "I'm-right-and-you're-wrong" dead end. A punishment boundary is communicating that your way is the only way. What you lose here is conflict's golden opportunity to address a real problem with a collaborative solution.

Example: After her husband forgets their anniversary, Maria gives him the silent treatment for a week because "my boundary is respect for important dates." She's not trying to collaborate on a better outcome in the future; she's trying to make him suffer for his mistake.

Example: When Jake's partner is 20 minutes late to dinner, he refuses to speak to her for most of their date because "my boundary is punctuality." He's using the boundary as an excuse for revenge, not protection of peace.

When we punish our partner for behavior we don't like, we miss an opportunity for constructive communication on what needs to change in the relationship. Or worse, we use this defensive boundary to avoid confronting a deeper problem. For instance, if you have to regularly "punish" your partner in the relationship, this could be an issue of compatibility. But facing your incompatibility could change *everything*.

Reality: Boundaries are used to protect your peace and values, not to punish others.

Example: "If you're more than 15 minutes late without communicating, I'll make other plans rather than waiting because I value my time."

Myth 3: Boundaries only apply to romantic relationships.

Boundaries are valuable in many aspects of life when you understand their purpose and apply them correctly. Although they are a handy and necessary tool within a romantic relationship, they can also serve you in other connections, for example, your relationship with your employer, your relationship with yourself, or your relationship with your children. When it comes to material experiences—anything happening outside your mind—there will always be things you cannot control, such as how your coworker speaks to you or how your children emotionally act out in public. Although we would like to believe we can control others, we cannot, and constantly fighting for the upper hand will leave you depleted and defeated. A boundary is a way to engage with those out-of-control situations in a predetermined way that gives you peace, clarity, and space. Your boundaries provide you with a road map of the only thing you can control: how you act in any given situation.

Reality: Boundaries are essential tools for every aspect of life where you interact with others or yourself.

Example: Emily's family constantly comments on her eating habits. Instead of trying to change their commentary, her boundary is: "When food comments start, I'll excuse myself from the table until the conversation moves on."

Example: When Michael's teenage daughter screams, "I hate you!" during arguments, instead of shouting back or punishing her, his boundary is: "When voices are raised, I'll pause the conversation and resume it once we've both had 30 minutes to cool down." He's not controlling her emotional outbursts; he's managing his own response to them.

Positive Boundaries That Work

What is a positive boundary, and how do you use it? So far in this book, you have begun the incredible process of rediscovering yourself, reevaluating your network, and getting honest about what you want moving forward in life and love.

> **Boundaries are where intention becomes action.**

Having big goals and high expectations for ourselves and others can be exciting. Still, your commitment to holding yourself accountable to the vision you've created will be a test of determination. Boundaries are the tool that keep you aligned with your goals and expectations.

Now that you know the type of partner you truly desire, you must not compromise on a relationship that will leave you feeling like you've settled or dismissed your needs, desires, or dreams. Compromising on your relationship standards is an all too familiar path that can lead to regret, resentment, and pain. By setting boundaries for yourself (note: not for someone else), you will avoid falling into that trap.

What Positive Boundaries Look Like In Action

Let me share a personal experience that shows how setting a clear boundary for myself protected my well-being during a challenging time.

REAL TALK: Breaking the Reaction Cycle

Near the end of my divorce, my ex-husband had already moved in with another woman, and less than four months later, she was pregnant. Needless to say, this was a lot to take in. I already found myself challenged trying to co-parent with him while knowing that he had spent the entirety of our marriage and dating life cheating and lying to me about it. Then I'd discovered he had spent the majority of our separation continuing to see other women, all while claiming he "wanted to work it out." Now he was having a child with the woman he had moved in with before even signing our divorce papers. Hearing this news felt like finally hitting the ground after being thrown off a hundred-foot cliff. I couldn't get lower. To top it off, this new woman did not like me and frequently took opportunities to tell me that.

Enter boundaries.

After two years of riding this emotional rollercoaster with my ex and now his new baby momma, I was exhausted. I was beaten up, and I was fed up. I was tired of spending my energy on this situation with him rather than on my son, my schooling, and my dreams and goals. So this was the moment I decided enough was enough. I needed to figure out how to keep myself from engaging in these same cycles of arguments, mud-slinging, and back and forth with the two of them, but how? The answer was simple, though not easy. I needed to set a boundary for myself. I needed a strategy to give myself time to respond to their provocations in a way that didn't drain me and further deepen the animosity in our co-parenting relationship.

The first boundary I set was the 24-hour rule. It worked like this: when I inevitably received a heinous, angry text from my ex or, more commonly, from his pregnant girlfriend, I would wait at least 24 hours to respond. This was a promise I made to myself to achieve my desired outcomes. Waiting a day didn't necessarily keep my darkest emotions from bubbling up when I read their messages. But I knew when reading them that I didn't have to, nor should I, respond at that moment, no matter how good of a snap back or "gotcha" I had on the tip of my tongue, because those impulses weren't serving me or my son. So, with this boundary, I gave myself time and space to allow those heightened emotions and thoughts to move through me and transmute into something more productive and less reactive.

As you can see, boundaries aren't about controlling others; they're about managing yourself in challenging situations.

Moving forward, get specific about what you want in every area of your life, not just romantic relationships.

> **Having standards and boundaries for your career, friendships, and even with yourself is a powerful way to live a life you love.**

Ask yourself: Do you feel valued, respected, and heard in your workplace? Do your friends build you up or break you down? Are you proud of the state of your physical health?

DIVE DEEPER: Setting Positive Boundaries

1. What areas of your life would benefit from boundary setting?

2. What standards or boundaries could you set to reframe the situations you feel powerless in?

3. What's one small step you can take this week toward living your values?

Bringing It All Together: Daring to Want More

Your desires and boundaries are the foundation for creating the life you truly want. Throughout this chapter, we've explored how to get clear about what you want and how to protect those goals through healthy boundaries. Remember, asking for what you want isn't selfish or unreasonable—it's an act of self-love and a crucial step toward creating authentic relationships. When you know your worth and own your desires, you naturally attract experiences and people that align with your vision.

KEY TAKEAWAYS:

1. *Authentic desires emerge from self-awareness, not external pressure or need.*
2. *Boundaries are used to protect your values, not control others.*
3. *Asking for what you want takes courage but creates clarity.*
4. *Your standards shape your future - choose them intentionally.*

Now that you finally know what you want, let's get it! In Chapter Six, "Dating Again," we'll take everything you've developed so far—your self-discovery, daily practices, and crystal-clear desires—and put them to work in the dating world. But this time, you won't be dating from a place of loneliness or need. You'll be stepping out there as the magnificent, self-aware person you've become, ready to attract the kind of love that only improves the quality of your life. Stay with me as we navigate the dating scene with fresh eyes, solid boundaries, and a secure mindset that empowers you to ask for exactly what you deserve.

BEFORE MOVING ON:

1. Write down an authentic desire that you've been afraid to admit to yourself or others.

2. Identify the specific obstacles (internal beliefs or external relationships) that have been preventing you from pursuing this desire.

3. Brainstorm boundaries that will protect your energy and help you commit to this desire – be specific about what you'll do when this boundary is tested.

- CHAPTER 06 -

Date Better

*Your relationship with yourself is the foundation for every other
relationship in your life.*

Congratulations! If you've made it this far, you've done the hard work of processing grief, investing in therapy, building better daily habits, rediscovering yourself, and getting crystal clear about what you want. Now comes the exciting (and maybe a little scary) part: putting it all into practice in the dating world.

In this chapter, we'll transform everything you've learned into action as you step into dating with authentic confidence and clarity. When you show up as this self-aware version of yourself, you naturally attract other emotionally healthy people—especially potential partners capable of the kind of relationship you deserve. If you've been sticking with this process and taking the necessary action, I imagine you're starting to feel connected to yourself again. Maybe you feel more secure or have a stronger sense of groundedness. This newfound vibrancy is special; knowing yourself better and feeling centered is the goal. If you stick with this, you will find yourself interested in dating again, and maybe, for the first time, from a position of wholeness.

In this chapter, we'll explore:
- *How to identify your true motivations for dating*
- *What secure dating looks like compared to insecure patterns*
- *How to reframe past relationship experiences to build confidence*
- *The power of radical honesty in creating authentic connections*
- *Practical tools for maintaining boundaries while dating*

Part One: Dating for the Right Reasons

Before diving into *how* to date differently, let's first clarify *why* you're considering dating again. Your motivation for dating will shape everything that follows, so starting here is crucial.

Reasons people start dating again

Not Recommended

- Feeling Bored
- Feeling Lonely
- Needing Affirmation or Validation
- Wanting Attention
- To avoid the thoughts and emotions that lead to real healing

Recommended

- Your goals for the future include finding a life partner
- You desire to share your authentic self with a romantic partner
- You seek to expand your personal growth through intimate connection
- You are ready to put what you learned from your past relationships to work
- You desire to set a healthy relationship example for your children

KEY INSIGHTS: The Root of Dating Readiness

- *Fear-based dating comes from scarcity.*
- *Desire-based dating comes from abundance.*
- *Your "why" shapes your results.*
- *Clear intentions create clear boundaries.*

The lists above aren't just theory; they're a practical tool for assessing your dating readiness. Looking at them side by side, you can see how each comes from a different motivation and creates an entirely different foundation for a relationship. Think of dating readiness like building a house: You wouldn't start putting up walls before laying a solid foundation. In the same way, you don't want to start dating before understanding your true desires and motivations. When we examine these contrasting approaches closely, we see two distinct relationship paths—one that seeks to fill emptiness from the outside and another that shares fullness from within.

Let's get clear about why you want to start dating again (if and when you do). I'm not saying your reason has to be on my list of recommended starting points; you may have your own even better and more personal reasons. The key factor I encourage you to consider before dipping back into the dating pool is how *secure* you feel. We'll cover this more in a minute.

Notice how some themes in the *Not Recommended* list are fear, avoidance, and apathy. Meanwhile, the *Recommended* list is more in tune with love, expansion, and curiosity. Why does this matter?

The motivation behind an action directly affects the result.

In other words, you will get back what you put in. If you are a bored partner, dating because you don't want to be alone, you are more likely to end up matched with someone who is dating you for the same reason, someone with unmet needs needing to fill a hole. Later when you can't figure out why the person you started dating out of boredom two years ago won't finally commit to you, the answer should be pretty obvious. You failed to set a clear intention from the outset of the relationship. Without clear intentions, there can be no clear boundaries or communication. Starting with all of these missing priorities already sorted will ensure the foundation necessary for a thriving relationship.

The other difference I haven't yet pointed out between the two lists above is their opposite root. Everything on the *Not Recommended* list is trying to fill a basic need. For example, there is nothing inherently wrong with needing affirmations or attention. But when you need those things from a partner because without them you are completely starved for validation, there is a bigger problem. You have not yet found a way to fill that need for yourself. And I'm not saying you're wrong to enjoy hearing compliments or affirmations from others; we all want them. I'm saying that if you are so starved of self-love that the only way you can meet your need for validation is through dating, then dating will only place a bandaid on that wound. No partner will ever be able to love you enough to fill that gap fully.

Relationships formed to help us fill *base needs* will fail.

Oppositely, reasons from the *Recommended* list are rooted in *desire*, not want or need. While wants often come from a place of lack or impulse ("I want that new car," "I want someone to text me back"), true desires emerge from your authentic self. They're those deep knowings that resonate in your heart—like the desire to create meaningful connections or to share your gifts with the world. These desires aren't reactions to what others have or what society tells you to chase. Instead, they're personal visions that expand your life and grow with you.

Some beautiful things about genuine desires are how uniquely personal they are and how they evolve alongside us. Maybe you previously envisioned yourself as the CEO of your own Fortune 500 company, but as you matured and separated your authentic desires from society's expectations, you now recognize you want a strong partner with whom you can build a loving family and beautiful home. You won't find yourself desperately grasping at desires the way you might chase wants. Instead, desires pull you forward naturally toward growth, inspiring rather than depleting you. At every stage of our life, we have desires that match the level of love, abundance, or success with which we are currently familiar. As we upgrade our lives, we can't help but upgrade our desires. In this way, our personal development reflects the beautiful, ever-expanding nature of the universe.

I invite you to look for evidence of this in your own life. At sixteen, many of us just wanted to buy whatever used car we could afford to gain a little independence or kiss that first love. But as a thirty-something professional, your greatest desire may be to upgrade your home, mindset, or investments. We now desire the kinds of things we wouldn't have even dreamed of at sixteen. The same expansion applies to our love lives.

As we grow and evolve and gain experience and insight into who we are and where we want to go, our desires for our partner become richer and more profound. Our wishes deepen and mature. You can go from being satisfied he texted you back to trusting someone so deeply you can safely place your heart in his hands! I hope this trust-based, affirmative desire is something I can help you cultivate.

By choosing a partner from secure desires rather than frantic needs, you will never date the same way again.

EXERCISE: *Dating Readiness Check-In*

Time needed: 15 minutes
Materials: Journal, pen

1. Review both lists of dating motivations

2. Honestly assess where you are right now:
   - Which motivations resonate most with you?
   - What fears might be driving you to date again?
   - What genuine desires are pulling you forward?

3. For any lack-based motivations:
   • How could you meet these needs yourself first?
   • What support might you need to feel more secure?

4. Journal about what dating from desire would look like for you.

Part Two: Dating From Security

How secure are you?

One of the first pains you will encounter when re-entering the dating world is rejection. Rejection can come in many forms; it can be the judgment you feel when you share your painful history with a new date or criticism from friends, family, or coworkers who have no idea what you're going through but have an opinion on how you're handling it. Rejection can even come from within, in the form of that little voice in your head that says, "Why even try this love thing again at this point? No one will choose me."

I say all this because I want you first to be mentally prepared for this growing pain. You are about to open up a door for yourself that may have been closed for a very long time, dating. Of course, there will be both fantastic and unwanted experiences behind that door. That's just life, and it's normal. So when things don't go your way, or you're feeling rejected or judged, the most empowering thing you can do is *not take it personally*. Being able to do this is the difference between secure and insecure dating.

As I mentioned at the opening of this chapter, we all share particular basic needs, and when we only look externally to fill them, we are often left disappointed. The beauty in learning how to fill these needs for ourselves *first*, in a patient and loving way, is that when we finally choose to date again, we are no longer looking for the bare minimum in a mate. We *enter into overflow*. We are already satisfied within ourselves, so everything else is just icing on the cake. So what does this look like?

REAL TALK: Security In Action

After my divorce, when I finally decided to try dating again, I met someone. We had a powerful physical connection, and he fulfilled many of the qualities I desired in a man and a partner. He could provide, we shared similar interests, and we naturally had fun together. However, there were some other things I knew could, and eventually did, become a problem, including his drinking. He was by no means an alcoholic, but he was a combat veteran who would use alcohol as a way to relax in the evenings and help him get to sleep. The old, insecure version of me was quick to push a familiar narrative. My thoughts went something like this:

> *If he likes me as much as he says he does, why can't he spend one night sober with me so we can actually connect? Am I not interesting or important enough? Maybe one day it won't be so bad, he's great in a lot of other ways, I shouldn't mess this up by pushing too hard. Maybe I can convince him to go to therapy.*

This line of thinking may sound familiar to some of you, and it is a very common internal struggle that many of my girlfriends and I have faced when it comes to dating.

Now I want to share how my secure self ultimately stepped in and handled the situation.

His drinking is something he is struggling with and may not even have control over. I know only he can fix this problem. I know I don't want to stay, wait, and hope his drinking will change. I need to be honest with him about how his nightly alcohol use makes me feel. And if he can't or won't change his drinking habits, I need to move on from this relationship and seek someone capable of building the intimacy I desire.

Can you imagine the two completely different paths of action these contrasting thoughts could take me down? The first would have kept me in a relationship that was not actually serving me or building me up. I would be left questioning if I was enough to motivate him to change, or I would have spent my energy trying to build this man into who I needed him to be. However, the second option empowered me to empathize with his struggle without making the mistake of thinking it had anything to do with me, all while still being able to advocate for what I wanted in a relationship.

KEY INSIGHTS: Secure vs Insecure Dating

- Secure dating means not taking rejection personally.
- Insecure dating tries to change others.
- Secure dating maintains empathy while honoring your needs.
- Insecure dating compromises your needs to keep or change others.

Now that you've seen how security plays out in real life, let's strengthen your secure foundation with a powerful reframing exercise.

Here is your challenge. Take a look back at your past relationships, not to criticize yourself, but to take stock of situations where you may have mistaken someone else's struggle as meaning something about you. Maybe your husband, like mine, was a serial cheater. Rather than believe this meant you were not attractive enough or a good enough wife, you can reframe that situation. You can separate *his struggle* to show up as the husband he promised to be from *your value* as a partner. Being able to separate your intrinsic value from someone else's behavior is a good way to start rebuilding confidence and showing up more secure for your next relationship.

EXERCISE: *Reframing Past Relationships*

Time needed: 30 minutes
Materials: Journal, pen, quiet space

Steps:

1. List 2-3 past relationships and identify where you took someone else's struggle personally

2. For each relationship, write:
   - What you thought their behavior meant about you
   - What their behavior actually revealed about their own journey

3. Dig deeper into your patterns:
   - How did your earliest experiences with love shape these interpretations?
   - What new perspective can you bring to these situations now?

If you want to take this reframing exercise even further, you can. Because of its formative nature, the love we experience from our parents in childhood sets our expectations for love in romantic relationships. Kind of gross, I know. But stick with me.

The importance of connecting childhood patterns to adult relationships is a hard lesson I learned when rebuilding after my divorce. I began to look under my own hood for the first time for the answers that can be hard to face. For instance, why did I stand by my ex for so long even though he had displayed untrustworthy behavior very early in our relationship, didn't make me feel safe, and was honestly not much fun to be around? I found the answers had a lot to do with the type of love I was shown or, rather, not shown as a child.

REAL TALK: *Lies About Love*

Through my younger years, my parents' behavior had conditioned me to believe that when someone loves you, they criticize and emotionally abandon you. Though I'm sure this conditioning was unintentional and likely passed down to them from their own critical and emotionally stunted parents, it created a toxic cycle of emotional neglect that would shape my understanding of love for years to come.

Take, for example, my mother's perfectionism. Chores were a minefield of impossible standards—cleaning a bathroom would take hours because my mom would meticulously check for "missed spots," ensuring I could never truly meet her expectations. Even the praise I received, for my grades, was used as a weapon. She would call my younger brother in to show him my straight A's, using my achievements as a tool to shame him for his academic struggles. In high school, when I suffered from depression and gained weight, my mom didn't offer support or ask what was wrong. Instead, she called me fat and threatened to ground me if I didn't walk on the treadmill for 30 minutes daily.

The constant criticism and impossible standards led me to believe that being put down was just a part of being loved, not feeling good enough was just a part of life, and expressing pain would only invite more punishment. Consequently, when I entered the dating scene, I attracted a partner who confirmed all these unchallenged narratives. My first husband's betrayal simply echoed what I already unconsciously believed—love is pain, and my worthiness of it is conditional and fragile. He didn't create this belief; he merely reflected back the script I had internalized since childhood.

I began to unpack and reframe the people, circumstances, and beliefs from my past that were haunting my relationships by asking hard-to-answer questions like: "Why didn't I see his betrayal coming?" and "Why did I put up with being treated that way for so long?" But here's the real gift—when you start understanding why you made certain choices, you start seeing others differently, too. Once I could look at my own self-sabotaging patterns with compassion and see how they stemmed from my unhealed wounds, suddenly I could extend that same understanding to others—even the ones who hurt me.

Now I can see that my mother was who she was because of the pain she endured in her life. Her inability to show affection and love me in the way I needed as a child didn't mean I wasn't worthy of that kind of love and affection; it meant she lacked the capacity to give unconditional, maternal love because she had never experienced it herself. I am able to see that my ex-husband's cheating was not a reflection of me as a wife or mother, but of his inability to be honest with himself about who he was and what he wanted. Of course he wasn't able to be honest with me.

Examining your childhood relationship patterns and their influence on your adult romantic choices is a challenging but rewarding exercise if you are willing to take it on. If you haven't already, start working these things out in a journal. And when you find yourself falling back into that place of taking things personally again or feeling stuck as a victim, go back and read what you wrote.

> **Wisdom comes from seeing people for who they truly are—broken and imperfect—and peace comes from understanding that their behavior reflects their own unhealed wounds, not your worth.**

Part Three: Dating and Radical Honesty

So now you've done the work. You have armed yourself with clear expectations and boundaries. You are feeling secure and ready to express your authentic self to someone new, free of frantic neediness or the fear of judgment or rejection. Essentially, you're finally happy just being with yourself, and now have the desire to look for another person who will bring overflow to the joy in your life and also inspire and challenge you to grow—freaking awesome, right?

Say you meet this amazing person in whom you see great potential, and they feel the same about you. How do you get a new relationship off on the right foot? How do you build a strong foundation that can stand the test of time and trust? The best and only way I have found to do this is with radical and upfront honesty. And if you're unsure what you should be divulging, what matters and what doesn't, you're welcome, because we already did that work!

Let's start by revealing the desires, expectations, and boundaries you built for yourself in the previous chapters.

Desires

Hint: These are exactly what they sound like.

So let's not overcomplicate the sharing of our desires. Often, as a way to skirt around the hard thing we don't want to do, we will remain in a state of confusion or, at least, feigned confusion, allowing ourselves to stay stuck. Sometimes being stuck is less scary than confronting a hard truth. The bottom line is that unless you feel comfortable telling your new or potential partner precisely what you desire, want, and expect, you will most likely never get it (or at least not get it consistently). Additionally, your partnership will always be on shaky ground because your partner, who presumably wants to please and satisfy you, will never have the tools to fulfill that mission, leaving you constantly disappointed. Such communication avoidance is no recipe for success, yet many people still wind up stuck in this broken relationship framework.

What am I proposing exactly? Radical honesty. And I don't mean in the mean-spirited, want-to-prove-a-point kind of way. I mean honesty in a self-reflective, peaceful and transparent kind of way. The act of this radical honesty can only ever result in one of two positive things. One, you learn something new about each other that makes the relationship better and deepens your intimacy to a new level. Or two, you discover something that reveals your incompatibility, freeing both of you to pursue relationships better aligned with your unique visions. What might feel like a loss in the moment becomes redirection toward the authentic lives you're each meant to live. These are truly the only possible results of honesty. Being honest is never the cause of our suffering.

> **Our resistance toward change, even when it's in our best interest, is where pain comes from.**

KEY INSIGHTS: The Power of Radical Honesty

- Honesty creates clarity for both partners.
- Confusion is often a way of avoiding hard truths.
- Every honest conversation leads to growth.
- Resistance to change causes more pain than honesty does.

Earlier in this book, I shared an example from my life where I was unyieldingly honest with my first serious partner after my divorce. Very early in the relationship, I opened up about my desire for my son to have siblings close in age and to have a family with someone I am in a committed, monogamous relationship with. I knew sharing my intentions would either reveal that he was not aligned with my goals and I would need to reevaluate our compatibility, or two, he would have similar desires to me and we could proceed together, confident in our shared vision. Perhaps you think being this radically honest means I either win or lose: If my partner rejects what I want, criticizes me for it, or avoids the subject altogether, then maybe I lose out on the relationship or the chance at a family. In the other instance, I win because I get what I want: the commitment to start building a family. But really, I get what I want in both situations because what I want is to not have to ever settle again for someone who is not aligned with my life's purpose. My desire is to only ever find myself in situations and with people who empower my ability to create the best life I can envision. This type of honesty will always guide who and where you should spend your time and invest your love, or if you want to continue settling, remain silent.

Boundaries

Whether communicating your preferences is easy for you or not, don't lose sight of the importance of saying what you need. If you haven't already taken the time to become aware of your boundaries in a relationship, do it now, or at least before you decide to start dating again. Having a plan on how you'll react to disrespectful or undesired treatment will bring clarity, prepare you to take action when needed, and allow you to protect your heart proactively. You will know how to take positive action without overwhelming emotion, confusion, or lashing out. Setting boundaries before a challenging situation arises will save you valuable energy in the long run. After all, you are your first line of defense against repeating past relationship mistakes.

At their core, boundaries in dating are your compass for authentic love. They're not walls you put up to keep people out, but rather signposts guiding you toward the relationship that fulfills your vision for love. Every time you honor a boundary—whether that's taking a pause before responding to a triggering text, or openly expressing when someone's behavior doesn't align with your values—you're saying, "I love myself enough to stay true to what I want." And here's the beautiful thing: when you consistently honor your boundaries while dating, you naturally attract connections that serve your growth and you filter out those that don't. As a result, you stop settling for less than you deserve, and you create space for the kind of love that adds to your life rather than depletes you. Remember:

> **your boundaries aren't just about saying "no" to what you don't want - they're about saying a big, wholehearted "yes" to the relationship you deserve.**

So as you step back into dating, let your boundaries be your guide. They'll never steer you wrong.

Action and Accountability

Once you know your boundaries, you must put them to use. Enforcing these personal standards can be challenging for those of us who aren't used to telling people what we want or are conflict-avoidant. But I don't necessarily mean making a list of your desires and deal breakers and going through each point on a first date. What I mean is remaining consistent with *yourself*. As we covered earlier, boundaries are not a tool to control or punish another person into being who you want them to be. They are a tool of *self-modulation*.

Say someone you are newly dating frequently trash talks their ex in front of you. Rather than rolling your eyes, accusing your date of not being over their ex, or pretending you don't hear them, you can set a clear boundary. You can directly address them and share how that talk makes you feel, hopefully opening up a productive line of communication. Or the next time they begin a rant, you can ask them to vent to a friend instead because of how listening to them bad-mouthing their ex is affecting you. Their interest in your comfort level will reveal volumes about their emotional maturity and respect for you. If they respond with care, you've found someone who values your feelings, and you've successfully advocated for your personal comfort; if they dismiss your boundary, you've gained valuable information about their character and can make an informed decision about what's in your best interest moving forward. You can also always excuse yourself from the situation until you are able to have this conversation calmly instead of blowing up at them.

I use boundaries to give myself buffer time before responding or reacting to something that has set me off, which has been a consistent tool of success for me. But knowing your boundaries without putting them into action will not accomplish anything, except maybe lead you to feel like you've let yourself down or are settling for less than you deserve. A great way to be sure you put your boundaries to work is with honest accountability.

I have already suggested some great tools you can use to hold yourself accountable and keep honest, things like journaling daily and surrounding yourself with people who have the same goals and dreams as you and want to support your rise to those dreams. The more you can consistently show up for yourself through these practices—the journaling, the walking, the therapy, the intentional circle of friends—the more you'll know you're not just going through the motions. You're actively creating the kind of life and love that once felt impossible.

The Relationship That Changes Everything

When doubt or pain inevitably tries to creep back in, my favorite question to ask is: "How can I love myself more?" The beauty of this question is that it gently guides you back to taking empowering action. That could mean you'll maintain your boundaries, recommit to your daily practices, show yourself some grace in the moment, or be radically honest about what you want. Maintaining a willingness to check in with and honor your wellbeing will always lead you in the right direction, whatever action you take.

I know firsthand how tempting it can be to self-abandon the moment someone exciting comes along. But here's an essential truth: Your relationship with yourself is the foundation for every other relationship in your life. You've come so far from those first raw days of heartbreak—days when you were hating your circumstances or feeling like an absolute failure. Now, you've learned to see your past through a lens of compassion, to set boundaries that protect your peace, and to embrace your deepest desires with unwavering conviction.

As you step back into the dating world, hold this close:

> **Your next great love story isn't just about finding the right partner—it's about becoming the right partner to yourself first.**

When you approach dating from a place of wholeness rather than desperation, everything shifts. The magnetic pull of your self-respect will ensure you never again settle for anything less than you truly deserve.

So go ahead. Take that leap. But this time, do it with the courage of someone who owns their values, the wisdom of someone who has healed, and the unshakable commitment to your most authentic vision.

FINAL REFLECTION: Your Journey

Time needed: 30 minutes
Materials: Journal, pen, quiet space, and your notes from previous chapters

Take a moment to reflect on your journey through this book:

1. Look back at where you started:
   - What were you feeling when you first picked up this book?
   - What did you believe about yourself and relationships then?
   - What were your biggest fears about dating again?

2. Notice your growth:
   - Which tools from this book have helped you most?
   - What new insights have you gained about yourself?
   - How has your view of relationships changed?

3. Look forward:
   - What kind of relationship are you ready for now?
   - What non-negotiables will you maintain?
   - How will you show up differently in your next relationship?

Afterword

*This is true freedom: not the absence of pain or challenges,
but the purpose found in them and the presence of something
greater than ourselves to help us carry them.*

Everything I've shared in the pages of this book—the tools, strategies, and practices—carried me through the trenches of my divorce. They were the best I had at the time, and they were effective. They helped me heal enough to move forward with my life and envision a future beyond my pain.

But this is about what came after—what I discovered once I'd climbed out of that pit. Something unexpected happened when I finally found myself in that new relationship I had dreamed of. My old wounds weren't as healed as I thought. My relationship trauma kept resurfacing, creating challenges I hadn't anticipated. I had healed enough to choose better for myself and my son, but once I had what I wanted, my fears kept creeping in, robbing me of the confidence to trust someone new.

I often found myself quietly comparing my new partner to my ex, scanning for red flags I felt I should have seen earlier in my first marriage. I constantly had my guard up—a wall between us—because the worst possible thing that could happen, the thing I absolutely had to prevent, was reopening my heart, only to be blindsided again. Although I had survived betrayal once, the idea of enduring it a second time made me want to crawl into a hole and never come out. This fear was paralyzing, and it left me resentful toward my ex for what he'd done but even more resentful toward myself. I was allowing those past painful experiences to poison my present happiness.

I once heard a powerful insight from a former semi-professional baseball player and coach. He explained something that stuck with me: when a player made a mistake or had a bad play, they were coached to literally look up. Keeping their heads down in defeat was proven to negatively affect their playing for the rest of the game. But if they looked up, they recovered from a bad play almost instantly.

This book ends where a new beginning emerged for me—one that required learning a different kind of strength. When I realized all my strategies and self-reliance had reached their limits, I faced a humbling truth: the strength I needed wasn't about how many good habits I could maintain or how well I could rationalize through my dark thoughts. It was about finding the courage to step into that unknown future I'd been dreaming of, not knowing if pain would come again, *but doing it anyway.*

This is how I came to find my greatest tool: Faith. Humbled by my own desperate insufficiency, I finally understood I didn't have to, nor should I, rely solely on *my* capabilities anymore. There was a higher power to draw from, one that loves unconditionally and never wastes suffering. Jesus said, "Come to me, all who labor and are heavy laden, and I will give you rest" (Matthew 11:28 ESV). That invitation, which I had heard countless times before, suddenly became my lifeline when I realized I couldn't do it all on my own anymore. I could lay down my intense fear of future "what ifs" at His feet.

I still do my part—practicing as many positive daily habits as I can manage while raising three children—but I also now draw power from something greater than my own strength and will. My newfound confidence comes from faith in a grander picture that, as I grow older, I'm more able to see and trust in its unfolding. It's the reason I can now be *grateful* for my ex and my divorce, because without the lessons gifted to me through that situation, I wouldn't be the wife, mother, and friend I am today, I wouldn't be writing this book, and there's not a thing I would change about any of that.

Acknowledging this divine design gives purpose to our most painful moments and redirects our minds—not to the fear of what was or what could be, but toward the reality that all of this is working for our good and the good of those around us.

Like those baseball players, I've learned to look up. In doing so, I've found that I no longer have to shoulder this burden alone. I've got an almighty God by my side—a support I wish I had surrendered to much earlier on this journey.

This is true freedom: not the absence of pain or challenges, but the purpose found in them and the presence of something greater than ourselves to help us carry them. I wish this place of rest for each and every one of you.

With love and hope,

Madison

Author Bio

Madison P Kirksey is an Air Force veteran turned transformational author who knows firsthand that heartbreak can become a catalyst for profound personal growth. After serving as a Chinese linguist and intelligence analyst for the National Security Agency and completing one combat tour in Afghanistan, she navigated single motherhood and divorce while pursuing her undergrad at San Jose University in Business Administration, ultimately discovering a system for turning emotional pain into power.

Drawing from her military background in intelligence analysis, Madison broke down the process of healing from heartbreak into clear, actionable steps that have helped herself and many close friends rebuild their lives after devastating loss. Her approach combines practical tools with deep emotional work, influenced by her journey from homeless youth to successful professional and devoted mother.

Today, Madison lives with her husband and three children, leading by example in creating the kind of love and life she once thought impossible. Through her writing, she empowers women to stop settling for less than they deserve and start building extraordinary relationships—starting with themselves.

When she's not writing or helping others transform their lives, Madison can be found practicing the very tools she teaches: taking mindful walks, journaling, praying, and spending quality time with her family. She believes every woman deserves extraordinary love, and she's made it her mission to help them find it.

Connect with Madison at: theauthormadison@gmail.com

Other Resources

Books:

EMDR:
Live Empowered! by Dr. Julie Lopez

Growth:
The Art of Happiness by His Holiness Dalai Lama and Howard C. Cutler
The Artist's Way by Julia Cameron
The Big Leap by Gay Hendricks
The Slight Edge by Jeff Olson
Mindset: The New Psychology of Success by Carol Dweck

PTSD:
The Body Keeps The Score by Bessel van der Kolk

Relationships:
48 Laws of Power by Robert Greene
Attached by Amir Levine and Rachel S. F. Heller
When Things Fall Apart by Pema Chodron

Journals:

The Five Minute Journal by Intelligent Change

Podcasts:

CBT/Thought Work:
The Unf*ck Your Brain Podcast with Kara Loewentheil

Thank You For Reading My Book!

Love this book? Don't forget to leave a review!

Every review matters, and it matters a lot!

Head over to Amazon or wherever you purchased this book to leave an honest review for me.

I thank you endlessly.

www.ingramcontent.com/pod-product-compliance
Lightning Source LLC
Chambersburg PA
CBHW062101270326
41931CB00013B/3168